Doing Corpus Linguistics

Doing Corpus Linguistics offers a practical step-by-step introduction to corpus linguistics, making use of widely available corpora and of a register analysis-based theoretical framework to provide students in applied linguistics and TESOL with the understanding and skills necessary to meaningfully analyze corpora and carry out successful corpus-based research.

This second edition has been thoroughly revised and updated with fresh exercises, examples, and references, as well as an extensive list of English corpora around the world. It also provides more clarity around the approach used in the book, contains new sections on how to identify patterns in texts, and now covers Cohen's statistical method.

This practical and applied text emphasizes hands-on experience with performing language analysis research and interpreting findings in a meaningful and engaging way. Readers are given multiple opportunities to analyze language data by completing smaller tasks and corpus projects using publicly available corpora. The book also takes readers through the process of building a specialized corpus designed to answer a specific research question and offers detailed information on completing a final research project that includes both a written paper and an oral presentation of the reader's specific research projects.

Doing Corpus Linguistics provides students in applied linguistics and TESOL with the opportunity to gain proficiency in the technical and interpretive aspects of corpus research and to encourage them to participate in the growing field of corpus linguistics.

Eniko Csomay is a Professor in the Department of Linguistics and Asian/Middle Eastern Languages at San Diego State University, USA.

William J. Crawford is a Professor in the Department of English at Northern Arizona University, USA.

Doing Corpus Linguistics

Second edition

Eniko Csomay and
William J. Crawford

Routledge
Taylor & Francis Group

NEW YORK AND LONDON

Designed cover image: © Getty Images | Punkbarby

Second edition published 2024
by Routledge
605 Third Avenue, New York, NY 10158

and by Routledge
4 Park Square, Milton Park, Abingdon, Oxon, OX14 4RN

Routledge is an imprint of the Taylor & Francis Group, an informa business

First edition published by Routledge 2016

Library of Congress Cataloging-in-Publication Data
Names: Csomay, Eniko, author. | Crawford, William J., author.
Title: Doing corpus linguistics / Eniko Csomay and William J. Crawford.
Description: Second edition. | New York, NY : Routledge, 2024. |
Includes bibliographical references and index. |
Identifiers: LCCN 2023039131 (print) | LCCN 2023039132 (ebook) |
ISBN 9781032425771 (hardback) | ISBN 9781032414713 (paperback) |
ISBN 9781003363309 (ebook) Subjects: LCSH: Corpora (Linguistics) |
Linguistic analysis (Linguistics)
Classification: LCC P128.C68 C74 2024 (print) | LCC P128.C68 (ebook) |
DDC 420.1/88—dc23/eng/20230828
LC record available at https://lccn.loc.gov/2023039131
LC ebook record available at https://lccn.loc.gov/2023039132

ISBN: 978-1-032-42577-1 (hbk)
ISBN: 978-1-032-41471-3 (pbk)
ISBN: 978-1-003-36330-9 (ebk)

DOI: 10.4324/9781003363309

Typeset in Sabon
by codeMantra

Contents

Tables

Figures

Preface

In our experiences teaching introductory corpus linguistics classes, we have found that undergraduate and graduate students gain both confidence and ability doing corpus analysis when they are given the opportunity to work with corpora and are exposed to hands-on experience with corpus tools and corpus analysis. While an understanding of the principles, approaches, and advantages of using corpora provides the necessary foundational knowledge of this approach to language analysis, there is a technical side to corpus linguistics that is best acquired through practice and experience with corpora. We have found that students are sympathetic to the benefits and advantages of using language corpora, but the real challenge is teaching them how to work with corpora. When "doing" corpus linguistics, students need to gain experience searching a corpus and interpreting the results of their corpus searches so that they can use this information to explain why their analysis and findings are important or relevant. In this book, we offer multiple opportunities to work on corpus projects by first including an entire chapter dedicated to smaller corpus projects (Chapter 4) and then providing students with information on how to build and analyze their own corpora (Part III). We have found that offering students the opportunity to build and analyze their own corpora gives them valuable experience in corpus building and sometimes even encourages them to build other corpora for projects outside of the class.

In order to allow the students to gain experience in "doing" corpus linguistics, we have intentionally limited the corpora and software used in the corpus projects. There are many different corpora available with different levels of public availability and numerous software programs that can be used for analysis (some free and some not). An extensive list of English corpora around the world is at the end of the book.

Each corpus and software program has its own idiosyncrasies and we have found that these different corpora and software programs are sometimes confusing to students who do not have access to the corpora and/ or struggle to learn one program or search interface in a corpus and then have to learn another. To address this issue, all of the projects in this book use the suite of corpora created by Mark Davies at Brigham Young University (http://corpus.byu.edu/). In this way, students can use the different corpora available on this site so they have multiple opportunities working with a single search interface. For the larger corpus project, we have focused on one free-ware program, AntConc, developed and supported by Laurence Anthony at Waseda University (http://www.laurenceanthony.net/software/antconc/). We acknowledge that the corpora and software used in this book are not the only ones, but we feel that they provide a strong foundation for corpus analysis and allow students to start "doing" corpus linguistics with these readily available and user-friendly tools.

Because a good deal of corpus work involves quantitative data analysis, we also included some elementary statistical information (Chapter 6) and tests (Chapter 7). Keeping with one of the guiding principles of this book, we see this introductory information as a way to have students learn the basics of analysis with the hope that they may apply this knowledge in other projects or learn more about more advanced statistical techniques that they can use in the future.

There are many different descriptive and theoretical frameworks that are used in corpus linguistics. We have selected one particular framework to guide the students in their interpretation of their corpus findings. Register analysis has strongly influenced our work and we believe that this approach to understanding language use is broad enough to encompass the various types of projects that students choose to do. In Chapter 2, we outline the basics of a register approach to language analysis and then ask students to refer to this same framework when building their corpus and doing their corpus study. We recognize the relevance of other descriptive and theoretical agendas but feel that focusing on a single approach provides students with more extended experience interpreting their corpus results and motivating the significance of their findings. Without knowledge and practice using a specific framework, we have found that students can be quite enamored with the "button-pushing" aspects of corpus linguistics at the expense of interpreting the results of their searches.

We also recognize the importance of reporting on research in a cohesive way. To this end, we have included material dedicated to the specifics of writing a research paper and presenting research (Chapter 8). Our goal in this chapter is to provide both students and teachers with some guidelines for how to demonstrate and present their specific research projects.

In the final chapter (Chapter 9), we ask students to consider more advanced types of corpus research with the hope that this book will serve as an introduction to the field and encourage students to pursue these ideas at a more advanced level and perhaps even impact the field in significant ways.

Acknowledgments

We would like to thank the following people who have influenced this book. We first acknowledge the work of Douglas Biber at Northern Arizona University and Susan Conrad at Portland State University. Their work in corpus linguistics and register analysis has strongly influenced this book. Also, Mark Davies at Brigham Young University and Laurence Anthony at Waseda University have provided free online corpora and tools that are vital to the structure of this book. Finally, we would like to thank our students in the previous corpus linguistics classes we have taught. It is through these experiences that we have seen the need for such a book.

Part I

Introduction to Doing Corpus Linguistics and Register Analysis

Chapter 1

Linguistics, Corpus Linguistics, and Language Variation

1.1 Language and Rules/Systems

While all humans use language to communicate, the ability to describe language is not nearly as advanced as our ability to actually use language. One defining component of the scientific study of language (i.e., linguistics) includes a description of how language works. Speakers of English are able to produce plural nouns that end in different sounds – we say *batS* and *bagZ*, not *batZ* and *bagS*. These same speakers can also produce plurals of nonsense words that we have never heard before – we would say *bligZ* and not *bligS*. Speakers of English also know that *We worked out the problem* and *We worked the problem out* are both acceptable sentences but *We worked it out* and **We worked out it* may not be equally acceptable (the latter is likely to sound strange to many native speakers of English). The fact that we can agree on these aspects of English related to the pronunciation of plurals and word order points to the fact that language, in many respects, is predictable (i.e., systematic). Such aspects are not only related to sounds and the order of words, but they are also related to how we might use language in different contexts and for different purposes. For example, we would not be likely to ask a professor for an extension on an assignment by saying: "Hey, man. Gimme an extension". Instead, we are more likely to make such a request by saying: "Would you please allow me to hand in that assignment tomorrow? I have experienced some personal issues and have not been able to fully complete it yet".

While it may be difficult to explain these particular aspects of the English language, native speakers apply these "rules" of language flawlessly.

DOI: 10.4324/9781003363309-2

In other words, one important component of linguistic description is to make implicit "rules" or patterns of language (knowledge we use) explicit (knowledge we can describe). It is safe to say that language users follow rules (and sometimes choose not to follow rules) for specific reasons even though they may not be able to explain the rules themselves (or even if we cannot agree on what a "rule" actually is). An important part of linguistic study focuses on analyzing language, describing, and in some cases explaining, what may seem on the surface to be a confusing circumstance of facts that may not make much sense.

When many people think of language rules, they may think of the grammar and spelling rules that they learned in school. Rules such as "don't end a sentence with a preposition" or "don't start a sentence with the word *and*" are rules that many people remember learning in school. Very often people have strong opinions about these types of rules. For example, consider the excerpt below taken from a grammar website on whether to follow the grammar rule of "don't split an infinitive".

> Even if you buy the sales pitch for language being descriptive rather than prescriptive, splitting infinitives is at the very best inelegant and most certainly hound-dog lazy. It is so incredibly simple to avoid doing it with a second or two of thought that one wonders why it is so common. There are two simple solutions.
>
> (1) "The President decided to not attend the caucus" can be fixed as easily as moving the infinitive: "The President decided not to attend the caucus". I'd argue that works fine, and not using that simple fix is about as hound-dog lazy as a writer can get, but split infinitives can be avoided entirely with just a bit more thought. How about:
> (2) "The President has decided he will not attend the caucus". What the heck is wrong with that?
>
> It's hound-dog lazy, I say. Where has the sense of pride gone in writers?
> (https://gerryellenson.wordpress.com/2012/01/02/to-not-split-infinitives/)

Examples such as these are not uncommon. One would only have to look at responses to social media comments or blog posts to find many more instances of people who have very strong opinions about the importance of following particular grammar rules.

So far, we have looked at "rules" as doing two different things: 1) describing implicit, naturally occurring language patterns and 2) prescribing specific, socially accepted forms of language. Although both descriptive and prescriptive perspectives refer to language rules, prescriptive rules attempt to dictate language use while descriptive rules provide judgment-free statements about language patterns. Both prescriptive and descriptive aspects of language are useful. When writing an academic paper or formal letter, certain language conventions are expected. A prescriptive rule can provide useful guidelines for effective communication. However, descriptive approaches can be useful in uncovering patterns of language that are implicit (as in the examples described above). Descriptive approaches can also be used to see how prescriptive rules are followed by language users.

The concept of language rules raises another interesting question: Why are these rules sometimes followed and sometimes not followed? Consider the prescriptive infinitive rule described above. Is it accurate to say that those who write *to not attend* are not following a rule? In some respects, this may be the case, but there is another – perhaps somewhat misunderstood – issue related to language that deserves some attention and serves as a basis for this book: the role of language variation. It is an incontrovertible fact that language varies and changes. The type of English used in Britain is quite different from the type of English used in the United States. The type of English used in Britain or the United States also varies from region to region or among people from different socio-economic classes. The type of English used 150 years ago in the United States is quite different from the type of English used in the United States today. Language even changes and varies in a single person. The study of language variation seeks to understand how language changes and varies for different reasons and in different contexts. There are different perspectives on how to investigate and understand language variation. The perspective that we will take is, as you can tell from the title of the book, related to an area of language study called corpus linguistics.

1.2 What Is Corpus Linguistics?

One way to understand linguistic analysis and language is through corpus linguistics, which looks at how language is used in certain contexts and how it can vary from context to context. While understanding variation and contextual differences is a goal shared by researchers in other areas of linguistic research, corpus linguistics describes language variation and use by looking at large amounts of texts that have been produced in similar circumstances. The concept of a "circumstance" or "context" or "situation" depends on how each researcher defines it. Corpus linguistic studies have frequently noted the general distinction between two different modes of language production – written language and spoken language. From a written perspective, one may be interested in contexts such as news writing, text messaging or academic writing. From an oral perspective, one may be interested in language such as news reporting, face-to-face conversation or academic lectures. Although text messaging and academic writing are both written, the purpose of text messaging is quite different from the purpose of academic writing and we would likely expect some degree of language variation in these different written contexts. The same may be said with face-to-face conversation and academic lectures: both are spoken but they have different purposes and consequently have different linguistic characteristics. More generally, we might also expect that spoken language (in all its various purposes and contexts) would likely differ from written forms of language. Spoken language does not generally have the same type of planning and opportunities for revision that we find in many types of written language. We will consider how different circumstances (or situational variables) can affect language use in the following chapter. But, before we do, we would like to briefly describe what we mean by a *corpus*.

A *corpus* is a representative collection of language that can be used to make statements about language use. Corpus linguistics is concerned with understanding how people use language in various contexts. A corpus is a collection of a fairly large number of examples (or, in corpus terms, *texts*) that share similar contextual or situational characteristics. These texts are then analyzed collectively in order to understand how language is used in these different contexts. The result of this analysis is a collection of language patterns that are recurrent in the corpus and either provide an explanation of language use or serve as the basis for further language analysis. One common method used in corpus research is to look at the environment of a particular word or phrase to see what other words are found (i.e., "collocate") with the reference word. While there are many different corpora available (see a selection at the end of the book), as an example, we will use the Corpus of Contemporary American English (COCA), which is a publicly available collection of over 1 billion words of text of American English (freely available at www.english-corpora.org/coca/), to investigate the use of two words: *equal* and *identical*.

In many respects, *equal* and *identical* can mean the same thing (two things that are similar to each other), and they are often taken as synonyms of one another. For example, we can use both of these words in a sentence such as: *These two students are equal/identical in their performance on the exam* with the same general meaning. If we were asked to define the word *equal*, we may use the word *identical* in our definition (and vice versa). However, if we use a corpus and look at how these words are actually used, a different picture emerges. COCA shows us that, although they may sometimes be synonyms, these two words behave very differently. We are more likely to use expressions such as *equal opportunity*, *equal rights*, and *equal protection* rather than *identical opportunity*, *identical rights*, or *identical protection.* We are not likely to talk about *equal twins* or *equal copies* but instead use the phrase *identical twins* and *identical copies.* A consideration of the words that follow *equal* and *identical* suggests that *equal* is more likely to modify abstract concepts such as *opportunities, rights,* and *protection* while *identical* is more likely to modify concrete nouns such as *twins, items,* and *houses.* Without reference to large amounts of texts, we would likely not be able to make such an observation. This is one example of how corpus linguistics can provide information about language use that can help linguists understand how language is used in authentic contexts.

Additionally, the corpus can inform us about frequency differences between *equal* and *identical* as shown in Table 1.1. The top five collocates of *equal* occur between 950 and 405 times in the COCA corpus and the top five collocates of *identical* occur between 417 and 20 times in the corpus. In other words, we can see that the word *equal* is more frequent than the word *identical* because the frequency of collocates shows a large difference between the two words. In fact, the word *equal* occurs 22,480 times in the corpus, and the word *identical* occurs 8,080 times.

In addition to information on collocation and frequency, a corpus will also allow us to examine the extent to which certain types of prescriptive rules are followed. Let us look at what a corpus might tell us about splitting infinitives. Earlier in this chapter, we saw that this rule can raise the ire of some people – to the point of associating some serious character flaws in those writers who do not follow it. The Corpus of Contemporary American English shows that we have examples such as *to better understand* (874 times in the corpus) compared with *to understand better* (94 times) and *to really get* (349 times) compared with *to get really* (151 times). Additionally, the sequence of words *to better understand* is most commonly found in academic writing while the sequence *to get really* is most commonly found in spoken language contexts. This evidence suggests that a strong prescriptive statement such as "don't ever split an infinitive" runs into serious problems when looking at actual language use. In fact, some examples of split infinitives are more frequent in formal academic writing;

Table 1.1 Common right collocates of "equal" and "identical" in the Corpus of Contemporary American English (COCA)

	First word right	Number		First word right	Number
Equal	OPPORTUNITY	950	Identical	TWINS	417
	RIGHTS	881		TWIN	247
	PROTECTION	733		COPIES	29
	ACCESS	485		ITEMS	27
	EMPLOYMENT	405		HOUSES	20

others are more frequent in spoken language. In other words, even though there are strong views on certain usage rules of English grammar, many of these rules may run counter to authentic examples of how language is used by reference to corpora. That is to say, the "rule" against splitting an infinitive is not always followed (i.e., there is variation in the application of the rule).

We have already seen a few examples of what corpus information can tell us. Now we will consider the defining characteristics of corpus linguistics as they will be used in this book. In a general sense, a corpus can refer to any collection of texts that serve as the basis for analysis. A person might, for example, collect examples of news editorials that are on a particular topic and refer to this collection as a "corpus". However, would we say that this person is "doing" corpus linguistics? In their 1998 book, *Corpus Linguistics: Investigating Language, Structure and Use*, Biber, Conrad, and Reppen define corpus research as having the following characteristics:

- it is empirical, analyzing the actual patterns of use in natural language texts
- it utilizes a large and principled collection of natural texts, known as a "corpus", as the basis for analysis
- it makes extensive use of computers for analysis, using both automatic and interactive techniques
- it depends on both quantitative and qualitative analytical techniques

(Biber et al., 1998: 4)

In our discussion above, we have already seen examples of the first two characteristics. Corpus linguistics is concerned with language that is produced for reasons other than linguistic investigation. Instead of using judgments or intuitions about language (or making up examples of language that illustrate a specific point), corpus linguistics relies on language that represents actual language use. In this sense, the language in a corpus is "natural" or "authentic" because it represents how language is truly used in a given context. For the second characteristic, we have already seen the benefit of referring to very extensive samples of language; there are certain patterns of language that are found only by referring to large amounts of language. However, it is also vital to include only those texts that represent how language is used in a specific context. For example, if one were interested in looking at the linguistic characteristics of face-to-face conversation, they would not want to include examples of spoken language found in academic lectures or political speeches. Even though conversation and lectures share a common feature of being spoken (as opposed to written), they do not share other important characteristics (such as purpose of communication and amount of interaction between participants). Thus, a specific corpus must be large but it must also contain texts of the same type (i.e., share certain characteristics). The concept of a text in corpus linguistics may be different from how you generally view a text. A text refers to any sample of language that is used for some authentic purpose. From this perspective, texts include language that has been written (such as newspaper articles, letters, and fiction writing) but also written representations of spoken language (such as face-to-face conversations, sitcoms, or academic lectures).

The third and fourth characteristics of corpus linguistics make reference to the importance of computers in the analysis of language as well as different analytical approaches. It would be difficult to imagine how one might use a 450-million-word corpus such as COCA without using a computer to help identify certain language features. Despite the large number of texts and the relative ease of obtaining numerous examples, a corpus analysis does not only involve counting things (quantitative analysis); it also depends on finding reasons or explanations for the quantitative findings. In Chapters 3 and 4, we will cover some of the specific directions we can explore in the corpus through software programs that allow for different types of analysis. It is important to remember that corpus methods do not just involve using computers to find relevant examples; these methods also focus on analyzing and characterizing the examples for a qualitative interpretation.

In addition to these four characteristics of a corpus, Elena Tognini-Bonelli, in her book *Corpus Linguistics at Work* (2001), also provides some useful ideas in defining corpus linguistics. She describes the differences between reading a single text and using corpus linguistic tools to investigate a collection of texts (i.e., a corpus). To illustrate this difference, we will make reference to one specific type of text: a newspaper article. A single newspaper article is generally read from start to finish so that the reader can understand the content of the text and relate it to other points of view on a given topic. In English, the text is read horizontally from left to right, and all texts from this perspective can be viewed as a single communicative event or act. If one were to compile a collection of 300 editorials and use a corpus approach to analyze these texts, the ways these texts are used are quite different. The texts in a corpus are not read from start to finish in a horizontal manner as with a single news editorial; instead, the texts are a collection of different (but related) events and are investigated not as whole but as fragments, in the sense that many examples of a single feature are seen in relation to each other. In this sense, the corpus is not read horizontally but is instead read vertically – many examples of a particular language feature are examined at one time.

A final point to consider when looking at corpus research relates to various views that researchers may have about corpus linguistics. Elena Tognini-Bonelli (2001) has made a distinction between "corpus-based" research and "corpus-driven" research. In a "corpus-based" approach, corpus linguistic researchers are guided by previous corpus findings or by specific issues concerning language use. That is, researchers have a very specific idea before searching the corpus as to what linguistic item they are looking for in a corpus. We have already seen an example of this with the split infinitive discussion above. In this case, the perspective on the perils of using a split infinitive was outlined in the article and this perspective served as the basis for our corpus investigation on how split infinitives are actually used. Given this prescriptive rule against splitting an infinitive, we decided to see what a corpus, i.e., text samples of a naturally occurring discourse, would tell us about how this rule is applied by language users. Other examples include any linguistic feature that we know that we want to search for, such as individual words or individual grammatical items. In all instances, however, we already had an idea a priori (before the fact) as to what we were going to search for in the corpus. The other approach to finding out about language use that Tognini-Bonelli has identified is through a "corpus-driven" method. In contrast to the method described above, researchers following a "corpus-driven" approach do not attempt to do corpus analysis with any predetermined or fixed set of search criteria; instead, they use specific computational methods to see what types of language patterns surface from the corpus. They extract those patterns from the texts and document them, after which they describe them and interpret them. Examples of research following this approach are collocation and lexical bundle studies. Lexical bundles are the most frequently occurring four-word sequences in a register. We cannot know ahead of time what the most frequently occurring sequences are. Therefore, we rely on special computer programs that can extract those patterns from the corpus for us. Researchers then analyze them grammatically (Biber et al., 1999) as well as functionally (Biber et al., 2004). Not only lexical items can be searched this way; grammatical features can be, as well. Typically, researchers look for co-occurring grammatical patterns in texts to characterize registers that way. We will describe this method briefly in the last chapter as a way forward to doing corpus linguistics. In these types of studies, however, we do not have one specific language feature in mind a priori.

1.3 Register, Genre, and Style – Is There a Difference?

Researchers in the field of applied linguistics, and more specifically, in discourse analysis, have defined and distinguished notions of register, genre, and style when it comes to text analysis. Biber and Conrad (2019) provide clear guidance on how these three approaches define their purpose, the analytical goals and the methods they apply to investigate text varieties (see Chapter 1 in their book). Based on their discussion, we provide a very brief overview just to clarify the differences. Let's start with acknowledging the fact that the same text can be analyzed from any one of the three approaches but the purpose of the analysis, and the goals and methods to analyze the text will be different. Biber and Conrad (2019) offer four defining characteristics, based on which they describe the three approaches: "Textual focus", "Linguistic characteristics", "Distribution of linguistic characteristics", and "Interpretation" (p. 16). As is described and shown in their table (Table 1.1, Biber & Conrad, 2019), the only difference along the four dimensions just mentioned between studies taking a register or a stylistic approach is how the interpretation is done. While linguistic "features serve important communicative functions in the register" in register studies, those "features are not directly functional; they are preferred as they are aesthetically valued" in studies of style (p. 16). All other characteristics are the same, namely, both approaches take a "sample of text excerpts", are interested in "any lexical grammatical feature" that are "frequent and pervasive in texts from the variety" (Biber & Conrad, 2019: 16, Table 1.1).

In contrast, genre studies differ from both register studies and studies of style in all of the four dimensions mentioned above. As Biber and Conrad in their Table 1.1 describe it: 1) Genre studies use "complete texts"; 2) From the linguistic point of view, they use "specialized expressions, rhetorical organization, formatting" as their main focus; 3) As for the distribution of language features, they focus typically on one particular feature as they occur in particular text positions; 4) Their interpretation of features is that they "are conventionally associated with the genre; the expected format, but often not functional" (2019: 16).

In this book, we take a register perspective to describe linguistic variation whether it is lexical, grammatical, or textual.

1.4 Outline of the Book

This book is divided into three main parts. In Part I, we introduce the concept of a corpus and locate corpus linguistics as an approach to language study that is concerned with the analysis of authentic language, and a focus on language variation, using large amounts of texts (Chapter 1). We then provide a register analytical framework for interpreting corpus findings (Chapter 2). In Part II of this book we focus on how to use existing corpora. We introduce a set of search tools and a set of language units that could serve as the basis for the analysis of already existing corpora (Chapter 3). We then provide 12 different projects that use existing online corpora in order to introduce the basics of how to work with corpora, interpret data, and present findings (Chapter 4). Once these basics of corpus analysis and an analytical framework have been addressed, readers will be ready to build their own corpora and conduct their own research study. Part III of the book takes you through the steps of building a corpus (Chapter 5) and then covers some statistical procedures that can be used when interpreting data (Chapters 6 and 7). Chapter 8 then provides a step-by-step process for writing up and presenting your research. Because this introductory book contains some of the basics of how to conduct a corpus research project, we do not cover many of the relevant issues that corpus linguistics is presently addressing in its research. In Chapter 9, we discuss some of these issues with the hope that this book has taught you enough about corpus research to pursue a more advanced study of the field.

References

Biber, D., & Conrad, S. (2019). *Register, genre, and style* (2nd ed). Cambridge University Press.

Biber, D., Conrad, S., & Reppen, R. (1998). *Corpus linguistics: Investigating language, structure and use*. Cambridge University Press.

Biber, D., Conrad, S., & Cortes, V. (2004). "If you look at …": Lexical Bundles in university teaching and textbooks. *Applied Linguistics*, 25(3), 371–405.

Biber, D., Johansson, S., Leech, G., Conrad, S., & Finegan, E. (1999). *Longman grammar of spoken and written English*. Longman.

Tognini-Bonelli, E. (2001). *Corpus linguistics at work*. John Benjamins.

Chapter 2

A Register (Functional) Approach to Language Analysis

2.1 Why Register?
2.2 What Is a Register (Functional) Analysis?
2.3 Describing Situational Characteristics and Identifying Variables
2.4 Providing a Functional Interpretation
2.5 Units of Analysis and Register Studies
2.6 End of Chapter Exercises

As we have discussed in Chapter 1, language variation is a prevalent characteristic of human language. There are, however, many different ways to investigate variation. We could choose to look at how language varies in different areas around the world (for example, the differences between British and American English). We could also investigate how language varies by identity or social class. Another way of looking at variation would be to consider the differences among individual writers or speakers. We could, for example, study the speeches of Martin Luther King Jr. in order to understand how his "style" might differ from speeches given by other people such as Winston Churchill. We could also take a different perspective and examine variation in language use by reference to the different contexts in which language is used. This approach can be done on both large and small scale depending on a specific research goal; however, at the foundation of this approach to language analysis is the assumption that language variation is functionally motivated by reference to clear descriptions of context. This perspective on language variation is referred to as register analysis which uses a series of steps to describe and interpret linguistic differences across relatively general contexts such as written versus spoken language or face-to-face conversation versus academic lectures. These same steps can also be used to describe variation in more specific contexts. Large-scale investigations require a representative (and usually quite large) sample of language and a method to determine linguistic features that are frequent in a given context. The research goal of this broad

DOI: 10.4324/9781003363309-3

approach to register analysis seeks to identify the linguistic characteristics of language used in general contexts such as face-to-face conversation or academic writing. More recently, similar methods used in the analysis of registers have been used to identify and interpret language variations that are not concerned with identifying and describing registers but are instead concerned with describing and interpreting language variation. This latter approach has been called a register-functional approach (Biber et al., 2022) and has been used to motivate empirically based studies of grammatical complexity (as opposed to identifying registers) but can also be used as to describe and interpret language variation. Both the broad and narrower uses are united by a shared perspective that linguistic variation is a) a fundamental characteristic of language use, b) dependent on contextual factors, and c) functionally motivated by reference to context. When we use the term register analysis, we are using it to include studies interested in the identification and interpretation of registers as well as a systematic way to interpret linguistic variation in texts that are not necessarily registers. In this chapter, we will take a closer look at the methods used to identify and interpret lexical/grammatical variation. The chapter will end by providing some examples of studies using register analysis and provide the reader with an opportunity to see how register analysis works.

2.1 Why Register?

As noted above, linguists have taken different approaches to investigate language variation. When traveling to different parts of the world, one may notice that there are different words for the fossil fuel that people put into their cars (*gas*, *petrol*, *motor spirit*). Not only do people have different words for things, but also the way that people say certain words can sound very different from region to region. In some parts of the United States, the words *pin* and *pen* both sound like *pen*. In some parts of the United States, people say *caught* and *cot* with different vowel sounds; in other parts of the United States, the words sound the same. The role that geographic location plays in lexical and phonological variation in these examples is generally covered in a field of linguistics known as sociolinguistics. Researchers in this field seek to understand how language variation is related to factors such as geographic region, identity, ethnicity, age, and socio-economic status. The traditional sociolinguistic approach frequently considers variation to be present when the same concept is expressed in different ways. From this standpoint, what counts as a variable must be a concept that is similar in meaning but different in the words used to describe it or in the phonological form of the word, or, in some cases, a different grammatical structure that describes the same concept (for example, the comparative structure *more better*).

Traditional sociolinguistic researchers will likely acknowledge that language doesn't just vary in the lexical, phonological, or syntactic form of similar concepts. Linguistic variation is not always the result of region or age differences but instead can be attributed to differences in mode (spoken versus written) or communicative purpose (informing versus persuading). Even within a specific mode or context, we find variation in specific written and spoken forms of language. Academic writing, for example, occurs in a different context than newspaper writing or letter writing. Viewing language variation in this way essentially "predicts" that contextual differences will result in the variation of linguistic features. In basic terms, a register is a variety of language that is characterized by both a specific context and the language used in the context. Variables in register analysis are not restricted to linguistic characteristics that are not meaning-changing; register analysis considers the context as a variable and looks at the different linguistic features that are found in specific situations.

In some respects, a register perspective is similar to traditional sociolinguistic approaches. Both sociolinguistic variation and register variation studies are interested in how social or situational characteristics relate to language use; however, register analysis considers a wider range of factors that are not only due to what are traditionally viewed as "social" factors (e.g., age, identity, socio-economic status). For example, when looking at potential differences between speaking and writing, the communicative purpose and topic are likely not as socially conditioned as are other components accounted for in register variation such as the relationship between participants. Seen from this perspective, register analysis takes into consideration a wider range of factors that may include social factors but may also include other factors, for example, topic, purpose of communication, and mode of communication. Another difference between sociolinguistics and register analysis relates to the linguistic features under investigation. Sociolinguistic studies are generally focused on a small number of language features that vary for purely social reasons. This approach allows us to understand why some people use the word *gas* and others use the word *petrol*. Register analysis takes a different view of language variation by using corpora to identify and interpret linguistic features. A register approach also uses a different type of analysis to investigate the extent to which linguistic features co-occur in given situations of use. From this perspective, the focus can either be on specific linguistic features or on the co-occurrence of multiple features found in particular situations of language use. Because register variation considers how linguistic features co-occur in a given context, a corpus linguistic approach is well-suited to register analysis because corpora provide large amounts of authentic texts for analysis. In fact, it would be hard to see how a register analysis could be achieved without the use of corpora. Looking at a smaller number of texts would likely not provide a representative sample of language use to allow for a characterization of a given register. However, as discussed above, the tools used in register analysis are also well-suited to identifying and interpreting variation in texts. For example, it is possible to look at two different types of writing tasks that vary in communicative purpose or in the amount of time provided to complete the task. The written text produced in two different conditions can be analyzed for variation in linguistic features and interpreted functionally. This is not to say that texts that vary in communicative purpose or time allotted to write a text are of different registers, but these contextual differences are likely to result in different linguistic features and that can be functionally interpreted. The number of texts needed for the latter approach does not necessarily have to be representative because the goal is not to identify a register but to provide a functional account of variation. The relevance of both applications of register analysis relates closely to the definition of corpus linguistics discussed in Chapter 1. Recall that corpus linguistics includes both quantitative and qualitative analysis. While the quantitative information can sometimes be fairly easy to obtain (after all, many times all one has to do is push a few buttons to obtain results!), proposing reasons for the quantitative information can be more challenging.

2.2 What Is a Register (Functional) Analysis?

If we see register as a variety of language, then we can describe register analysis as a framework to understand language variation. Register analysis is most readily associated with the work of Douglas Biber and his colleagues and students. According to Biber and Conrad (2019), a register analysis has three main components: 1) an analysis of the context in which a text is produced; 2) an analysis of the linguistic features that are found in the texts; 3) a functional interpretation of the relationship between the context and the language produced in a given context. This type of analysis illustrates systematic aspects of variation by showing how different contexts (called situational variables) relate to different forms of language (called linguistic variables).

As we touched on in Chapter 1 and will explore further in Chapter 9, scholars are typically interested in taking one of two approaches to study variation using corpus methods. On the one hand, they focus on variation in the use of one individual lexical unit (e.g., words, collocations, n-grams, or lexical bundles) or in the use of an individual grammatical unit (e.g., subordinate clauses, modals, pronouns). They use a corpus to find out how these individual features vary across contexts/registers. On the other hand, scholars such as Biber and his colleagues are interested in describing language variation from another point of view. Instead of focusing on individual linguistic features, they are interested in characterizing texts from a comprehensive linguistic perspective. To do this, they search multiple linguistic variables at the same time in a corpus. These studies report on how these multiple linguistic features work together (i.e., how they co-occur) in texts, and then examine how their co-occurrence patterns vary in the different registers/contexts. This approach provides a comprehensive linguistic picture of the text under consideration and allows for a functional interpretation of the relevant linguistic features.

Following the three components of register analysis described above, we focus on describing situational variables in this chapter. In Chapter 3, we will show you how to search an existing corpus for the linguistic variables you may be interested in (whether lexical or grammatical), and in Chapter 4, we will take you through several projects that will help you learn how to do studies of this kind.

2.3 Describing Situational Characteristics and Identifying Variables

Prior to any linguistic analyses, register studies examine multiple aspects of the communicative context (often referred to as the "speech situation") that the sample texts are taken from. During the past few decades, a number of scholars (e.g., Hymes, 1974; Halliday, 1978; Duranti, 1985) studied and discussed the nature of a communicative context, taking different perspectives on what constitutes the components of a speech situation. Mode is one aspect, for example, through which language used in these contexts could be described. Accordingly, spoken and written modes are considered very different and register studies have illustrated the ways that the language used in these two modes is drastically different.

Biber and Conrad (2019: 36–48) have identified the following basic components through which the situational characteristics of registers could be described:

1) Participants
2) Relations among participants
3) Channel
4) Production circumstances
5) Setting
6) Communicative purposes
7) Topic

Figure 2.1 provides an overview of the situational framework and provides some examples of each of the seven components. Although the specific examples of each component are not exhaustive, the figure and the following

Figure 2.1 Situational variables

short description of each component should help you to understand the range of factors that are considered in a situational analysis.

The first two factors that we will discuss are those of participants and the relationships between the participants. Participant information from a situational perspective includes who is doing the writing/speaking (the addressor) and who is doing the reading/listening (the addressee). There are many possible configurations of participants: in an academic lecture, it is generally the case that there is a single person lecturing to a larger group of people; in a panel discussion, there may be a group of people that are addressing another group of people; in face-to-face conversation there may be a single addressor and addressee or, in the case of a lively family discussion at the dinner table, there may be multiple addressors and addressees at the same time. Additionally, there are also times where an interaction may include people who can hear what is being said even though they are not actively part of the conversation – for example, those sitting on an airplane and listening to the conversation of others around them. In addition to the participants themselves, another relevant situational factor includes the relationships between the participants. Does one person have more knowledge about a topic than another? Does one person have a higher or a lower level of status or power than the other person? Are the people strangers, co-workers, or family members? Answers to these questions will likely have an effect on the type of language that is used.

In addition to participant information, a situational analysis also requires a description of the environment and conditions in each context. Relevant in this aspect are the channel and the production circumstances. Channel refers to both the mode and medium of the language. Mode refers to the way the language is transmitted: speaking and writing are generally the two main modes of using language, but there are also gestural systems such as signing that can convey meaning. Medium refers to the relative permanence of the language. We may compare many forms of written language as being more permanent than many forms of spoken language. Written forms of language can be preserved for multiple readers or multiple opportunities for reference while spoken language is generally more short-lived. This is not to say that all written forms of language are permanent, or all spoken forms of language are transient. We need to differentiate between mode and medium to distinguish the differences between a written grocery list and a recorded speech. The grocery list may be written out, but it is not as permanent as a recorded speech. In addition to channel, a situational analysis also characterizes the conditions in which the language has been constructed. We may also want to use mode and medium when referring to different types of written language found on the internet or cellular phones (such as social media posts, tweets, and text messages), which vary in grades of permanence depending on the topic and potential effect they have. We likely can think of examples when a writer has either deleted or regretted a particular tweet, social media post, or text message. The production circumstances of language may also relate to the process of planning, drafting, and revising. Some types of written or spoken language require extensive planning, drafting, or revising while other forms do not. In the written mode, an academic research article has gone through an extensive planning, drafting, and revising process; in a social media post or text message, generally this is not the case. Even in the spoken mode, we can acknowledge the differences in planning between an academic lecture or business presentation and face-to-face conversation. We can see the effect of production circumstances in spoken language where it has been shown that planned discourse contains fewer filled pauses (*uh, um*) and hesitations than unplanned discourse (Biber et al., 1999).

Next, we will take a closer look at the variables of setting and communicative purpose. Setting describes the time and place of the communicative events. A face-to-face conversation involves a shared physical space but may take place in a private or public setting. A telephone conversation may also be in a private or public setting but generally does not take place in a shared physical space. Another relevant variable related to setting includes whether the language has been produced in the present or in the past. For example, newspaper articles written in the 21st century are very different from those written in the 19th century. In addition to setting, variation also can be the result of the communicative purpose. In some contexts, the purpose is to inform, persuade, or tell a story while in other contexts the purpose may be to just interact and share thoughts, ideas, or feelings. There are also cases where we would expect that the language would be more or less factual. We would hope that a newspaper article or academic textbook would contain factual information. We generally do not expect facts in a fairy tale or work of fiction. Communicative purpose also includes the extent to which the speaker or writer uses language that expresses their attitude about the topic (something we might not expect in news reporting but might expect in a news editorial).

A final aspect of the situational analysis relates to topic. This is a very broad situational variable that has not been investigated in much detail. A conversation about where to find a suitable place to eat will likely have very different linguistic characteristics than a conversation about how to fix a broken refrigerator. In a similar way, an introductory psychology textbook will likely have very different linguistic characteristics than an introductory music theory textbook. However, the situational variable of communicative purpose sometimes is also relevant in relation to topic. One might argue that the communicative purpose of a conversation on finding a place to eat and fixing a refrigerator are quite different, but the two different textbook types share the same communicative purpose. Thus, topic and communicative purpose sometimes "overlap" or share relevance, but other times they do not.

Although we have covered seven different situational variables, there are cases in which all seven variables are not involved in a situational analysis and there are cases where additional aspects of the situation will need to be added. In a register analysis of potential differences between different types of news writing, many situational variables associated with participants, mode, channel, and production circumstances may not differ although the communicative purpose may. Editorial news writing often seeks to persuade readers to adopt or at least consider a specific viewpoint; news reporting does not share this same communicative purpose but instead seeks to inform readers. To examine the language of university classrooms as a context for a speech situation (or domain), we might need to consider discipline, level of instruction, or other aspects such as interactivity, as part of the situational analysis.

In Chapter 3, you will have the opportunity to do situational analyses in some of the projects, and in Chapter 5 you will do a situational analysis of your own corpus. To understand how to apply the situational variables to different text types, we provide three examples of situational analyses below.

2.3.1 Email to a Friend and Email to a Boss

There are at least three situational differences between a letter to a friend and a letter to one's boss: certain aspects of the relationship between participants and certain aspects of the production circumstances (see Table 2.1). Unlike the boss–employee relationship in which the boss has more authoritative power over an employee (i.e., there is a power differential), the relationship between friends does not have this same type of power differential (at least we would hope it does not!). At the same time, for other situational characteristics such as production circumstances or mode, they will remain relatively the same because they are both in writing. Yet, it could be that the text will be more carefully planned, revised, and edited when an email is composed to a boss or that the communicative

Table 2.1 Key situational differences between an email to a friend and an email to a superior (boss) (Biber & Conrad, 2009: 65)

	Email to a friend	Email to a boss
Participants	One author addressing one reader	One author addressing one reader
Relations among participants	No interaction	No interaction
	Author and addressee have the same knowledge	Author and addressee have the same knowledge
	Author and addressee know each other well	Author and addressee know each other
	Equal relationship, personal	**Unequal relationship, professional**
Channel	Written	Written
Production circumstances	Text **planned, may be edited, may be revised**	Text **carefully planned, edited, and revised**
Setting	Participants not in same physical space	Participants not in same physical space
Communicative purpose	Convey information; **share personal information/ updates**	Convey information
Topic	Varied	Varied

purpose of an email to a friend may not be the same as an email to a boss. As we compare these two registers situationally, the "linguistic features will mark particular components of the situation" (Biber, 1988: 28), and so the differences in language use could be attributed to the differences in the situational parameters.

2.3.2 News Writing and News Talk

In this section, we will look at two related contexts that also differ in some situational respects: news writing and news talk show language. While both of these texts share the situational characteristic of conveying (potentially new) information to an audience (under communicative purpose), there are many differences in other areas of situational analysis. Even the communicative purpose could be argued to be different in these situations in that the news talk show involves not only providing information but also presenting an opinion.

2.3.3 Classroom versus Symposium Presentations

Csomay (2015) explored the language of presentations in academic contexts. She started with the situational analysis of two contexts: classroom presentations and symposium presentations. While the channel (spoken),

Table 2.2 Situational differences between news writing and news talk

	News writing	News talk show
Participants	One addressor, multiple addressees	One addressor, multiple addressees (although the discussion is in the studio, the television audience is an "unnamed" addressee)
Relations among participants	Interaction between addressor and addressee **not possible**	Interaction between addressor and addressee **possible**
Channel	**Written**	**Spoken**
Production circumstances	Text **has been edited**	Text **may be edited on the spot**
Setting	Addressor and addressees **are not** physically in the same room	Addressor and addressees **are** physically in the same room
Communicative purposes	Convey information to the audience	Convey information to the audience **Provide opinion; express suitability for a position**
Topic	Varied	Varied

the setting (participants sharing the same physical space), and the over-arching communicative purpose (inform or expose to information) is similar in both contexts, there are important differences in other aspects of the situations.

More specifically, the main differences between the two situations shown in Table 2.2 are related to a) participants; b) relations among participants; and c) production circumstances. First, the social characteristics of the participants differ in the two contexts. In the classroom, the presenter is an expert professional, while at the student symposium, the presenter is a novice, or an emerging professional.

Second, the most pertinent differences are apparent as we examine the relationship among participants. For example, while classroom settings most likely allow questions at any point in time during the teacher's presentation, presentation settings have set routines and questions can only be asked after the presentation has been delivered. In terms of the presenter's familiarity with the participants, it is clear that the teacher knows (or is at least familiar with) most of the participants in the classroom because the same set of people would meet weekly for 12 or more weeks at a time in the same physical space. In contrast, the presenter at the student symposium may or may not know the audience. Yet another difference in this area is the presenter's social/academic status in the group they are presenting. The teacher (addressor) in the classroom setting is superior to the audience (addressee) and has a high social/academic status in the community. In contrast, the presenter at the student symposium plays a subordinate role in the academic community (especially if teachers are sitting in the audience) and has a relatively low social status in the community. If the student is an undergraduate, s/he has an even lower status than that of graduate students. If the student is a master's student, s/he will have a lower status than a doctoral student, and so on. Finally, the teacher holds the power in the classroom while the audience holds the power at this particular symposium because the presenters are being judged for their performance.

Third, the production circumstances are also different in the two settings. Primarily, this difference is attributed to the ability of instantaneous revisions of the text. In the classroom, there is plenty of room to negotiate and revise the text on the spot since questions can be asked at any time and clarifications can be requested. At the symposium presentation, there is a lack of spontaneous interaction, or immediate requests for clarification; there is no room for immediate negotiation of the text. Clarification questions can be made after the presentation has been delivered. Table 2.3 summarizes the aspects we have discussed so far.

In sum, there are enough situational differences in some of the aspects of this context to predict that language would be used differently.

Table 2.3 Key situational differences between student presentations at a symposium and teacher presentations in the classroom (adapted from Csomay 2015: 4)

	Classroom presentation (Instructor)	Symposium presentation (Student)
Participants	One addressor, multiple addressees	One addressor, multiple addressees
	Social characteristics: **expert** professional	Social characteristics: **novice** professional
Relations among participants	Interaction is possible **during** presentation	Interaction is possible but **only after** presentation
	Addressor has more knowledge than audience	Addressor has more knowledge than audience
	All participants have some specialist knowledge	All participants have some specialist knowledge
	Addressor gets to **know** most or all participants	Addressor **does not know** most or all participants
	Social/academic status of addressor is superior to addressee (**high status**)	Social/academic status of addressor is subordinate to most of the addressees in the audience (**low status**)
	Power is held in **addressor's** hand	Power is held in **addressee's** hand (judges evaluate performance)
Channel	Spoken	Spoken
Production circumstances	Text has been planned and may have been revised or edited prior to production	Text has been planned and may have been revised or edited prior to production
	Text **can be** negotiated, and revised on the spot	Text **cannot be** negotiated, revised, or edited on the spot
	Text can be read out	Text can be read out
Setting	Addressor and addresses are physically in the same room	Addressor and addresses are physically in the same room
Communicative purposes	Convey information potentially new to the audience	Convey information potentially new to the audience
	Explain concepts and methods	**Report on the procedures and results of a project**
	Comprehension by addressees is **not assumed**	Comprehension by addressees is **assumed**
	Convey personal attitudes	
	Direct students what to do	
Discipline	Varies	Varies

2.4 Providing a Functional Interpretation

The third step in a register analysis requires the researcher to provide a functional reason for the linguistic features in a given text. Because register analysis seeks to describe the relationship between situational variables and linguistic variables, the occurrence of linguistic features requires a description of the context. In fact, from this perspective, language features occur because they are fitting to a specific context. In other words, the situational variables in a sense "lead" language users to adopt particular linguistic features. As we discussed in the previous section, these linguistic features can be single features, but they can also be a set of co-occurring features.

2.4.1 News Writing and News Talk

In this example, we will show a single feature analysis focusing on first person pronouns in the subject position.

In Table 2.4, the text length is fairly similar (the news writing text contains 134 words and the news talk text contains 128 words); however, they differ in the number of first person pronouns, with two in the news writing text and six in the news talk. What situational characteristics might account for this difference? One possibility can be found in the communicative purpose. Because the participants in news talk shows are often asked to present their opinion (and in this particular case, make a case for why one political candidate is preferable over another), we would expect that a personal opinion (stance) would be expressed by referring to oneself as well as by including verbs such as *think*, and that suitability for candidacy would be expressed through verbs such as *can* and *have*. Another relevant contextual variable is related to the mode of production. In the spoken mode, people often refer to themselves (and others) in the conversation. Further support for this is found in the news writing excerpt where the two instances of a first person pronoun occur in a direct quotation. This short analysis does not mean that first person pronouns do not occur in written contexts, but we would not expect them to occur at the same frequency nor for the same reasons.

2.4.2 Classroom Versus Symposium Presentation

In Table 2.5 we show you a multi-feature analysis of two presentation types (analyzed above for the situational characteristics).

In these segments, we would like you to see differences in terms of the use of nouns and grammatical features specific to conversation such as non-clausal units, tags, and so on (Biber et al., 1999). We have italicized the nouns in each segment, and bolded and italicized the grammatical features specific to conversation. Just by looking at the patterns of the italicized features, we can see a difference. If we do the calculations, it turns out that the classroom text segment has 17.19 nouns and the symposium presentation text segment has 19.50, and the classroom text has 6.37 "conversational features" while the symposium presentation has 2.07.[1]

Table 2.4 Texts for news writing and a news talk (COCA)

News writing	News talk show
A playwright hikes into the woods with his laptop, works until the battery runs down and then hikes back. A theater company sets up huge pieces of scaffolding that double as musical instruments. An author sits in a cabin, working on a new play, wearing nothing at all. "When *I*'m in New York, there are neighbors across the way, " says Cassandra Medley, the playwright who takes au naturel to heart. "*I* just like to shed and think and feel." The opportunity to return to a "primeval, primordial" state is one reason that Ms. Medley—and other authors—love attending the growing network of summer retreats where writers and others who work in the theater get away from the urban grind and try to reconnect with their muses.	A: Except that Obama is likely to give it to them. *I* mean, that is the case. They're expecting Barack Obama to inject the enthusiasm into the Republican base. B: One of the great phrases that has been used in defense of venture capitalism and Bain Capital is Schumpeter's creative destruction. Whenever *I* hear Republicans say that, *I* want to say, you know what America has been looking for five years at a lot of destruction, creative and non-creative. They're not going to like that defense. They're going to like a defense that says, guess what, *I* can create jobs, *I* have a plan, we can move this thing forward, we can save our country. Treatises on the essential nature of capitalism, *I* think, won't do it for Mr. Romney.

Another type of analysis could tell us about the lexical density of the two texts. This is typically measured by the text's type-token ratio.[2] The higher the ratio, the fewer repetitions occur, generally indicating a more lexically dense text. In the classroom text, we have 157 words (tokens) and 102 types of words, so the type-token ratio for the classroom text is 157 / 102 = 1.54. For the symposium text, we have 241 words (tokens) and 116 types, so the type-token ratio is 241 / 116 = 2.07. This number simply means that in one text there seems to be more repetition than in the other text.

The question is: "Why are these two texts so different in their noun and conversational features and in their lexical density?" In other words, what may account for the differences? If we look at the situational differences between the two texts, there are many. However, perhaps most pertinent to these two segments is the production circumstances and the communicative purpose. In the classroom, there is no pre-set script to follow; that is, there is always room for asking questions, and the potential for interaction is always present. In contrast, at a symposium presentation, the rules are strict, and questions may be asked only at the end of the talk. Therefore, the presenter is expected to talk continuously for a period of time, after which the questions from the audience may be asked.

Table 2.5 Texts from a classroom presentation and a symposium presentation

Classroom presentation by teacher	Symposium presentation by student
So what I'm suggesting to you then, is, is that this second *dynamic*, which accounts for the *popularity*, the contemporary *popularity* of *civilian review*, has to do with *money*, and civil *liability*, and the *ways* in which the *behavior* of *law enforcement institutions* can, render, *municipalities* liable for millions and millions and millions of *dollars*, **uh**, in, **uh**, civil *liability lawsuits*. Not only that, usual *contingency*, **um, uh**, *rules*, are waived in these kinds of *lawsuits*. **All right?** What that means is that usually, when you pursue a civil *claim*, against somebody, you ask for a hundred thousand *bucks*, **OK**? And, you get it, and your *lawyer* takes a third. **All right?** What happens if you sue a *municipality* and they say yeah we think you're right but [short laugh] the *situation* was so much more complicated, we award, one *dollar*, **OK?** Is your *lawyer* gonna take thirty three cents? or in these kinds of *lawsuits*, **right?**	And we found that an immature *cynofields* resides in the *kidney* that's where we found the most *cells* with those *characteristics* and I interpreted that we found also **oh** . . . **oh** . . . a *relationship* for those *cynofields* but those were more mature. We can say that because . . . The *electro-microscopy results* with that we can see the *morphology* and *chronology* and this is a human *cynofield* with a *transmission* electronic *microscopy* of the human *cynofield* and we did with a *zebrafish* we found very similar *morphology* that *granules* are round as same as the human *ones* and the *nucleus* is big at this *stage* so we found the *cell* that looks like *cynofields* so now we want to study its *function* we study the *function* by *migration* of *recommendation* to the *infection* and then we see they change their *morphology*. So we know that *cycles-sum* in human *cynofields* includes *information response* and we inject the *fish* with the *cycles-sum* we let them live for 6 *hours* in order to provide an *order response* and then to (syll) we sacrifice the single *cell suspension* and within the *facts analysis* of *photometry* and those are our *results*. We found we use a *control* also and we can see in the *control* the *populations* of *cynofields* are in not increase as dramatically with the one that we injected we cycle-sum and it was 20% more of *population* of those *cell* that we found in this *gate*.

In terms of communicative purpose, there are two major areas that may account for the differences. On the one hand, in the classroom, the purpose is to explain concepts and methods; at the symposium, the purpose is to report on the processes and results of a research project. In addition, in the classroom, the addressor (the teacher) periodically checks for comprehension to see whether the students are understanding the material. In contrast, at the symposium presentation, the addressor (the presenter) assumes comprehension and expects questions to be asked afterwards. For these reasons, there seems to be quite a difference in the frequency of the conversational features between the two texts. However, the same is not true for the use of nouns. Because the communicative purpose in both contexts is to convey information that is potentially new to the audience, the actual information seems to be packaged in similar ways; that is, the information is delivered through nouns either embedded in noun-noun sequences or in a series of prepositional phrases. In terms of how the information is conveyed, we see differences in the type-token ratio. The teacher uses more repetitions (hence the lower ratio number) while the presenter is conveying the information without that many repetitions.

2.5 Units of Analysis and Register Studies

As we mentioned at the beginning of the chapter, many corpus researchers choose to investigate a single linguistic feature to see its variation in multiple registers. Among the lexico-grammatical studies is Fortanet's (2004), which, taking the Michigan Corpus of Academic Spoken English (MICASE), looks at the use of pronouns in academic lectures. More specifically, Fortanet classifies "we" into functional categories, which she then tracks to see how more or less interactive classes use this particular pronoun and their associated functions differently. Another example is found in Wulff et al. (2012), which examines the Michigan Corpus of Upper-level Student Papers (MICUSP) to describe "attended" versus "un-attended" *this* in student writing. Wulff et al. look at sentence initial uses of *this* and classify them first based on their part of speech category (whether they are pronouns taking the full noun phrase slot or they take the determiner slot in the noun phrase). Then, they investigate the frequency patterns of these two types of *this*, associate them with communicative functions, and look at their functional distributions. Because these studies considered the distribution of a single feature in different contexts, would this be included in register analysis? Although perhaps not everyone would agree, we tend to see these as examples of register analyses because they 1) make reference to specific situational contexts, and 2) provide functional reasons for the different uses of specific words. In fact, part of the value of these studies is found not necessarily in the frequency counts of a particular word but in the frequency of different types of functions in single words. For example, in Wulff et al. (2012), the lexical word *this* was associated with two different functions, so it was the frequency of the function that varied across texts rather than the frequency of the word *this*.

Another example of single feature analysis in corpus studies is found in studies focusing on two- or multi-word sequences (collocations, and n-grams or lexical bundles, respectively). Lexical bundles are the most frequently occurring word combinations in a register; that is, in situational language use. The most often investigated bundles are four-word combinations. Biber, Conrad, and Cortes (2004) investigate lexical bundles in university language use based on the T2KSWAL corpus (Biber et al., 2002) and classify them based on their grammatical characteristics and their discourse functions. Biber et al. (2004) specifically look at the distributional patterns of the identified bundles in two sub-registers within the university setting – namely, teaching and textbooks. Csomay (2013) takes this set of bundles and places them back into the discourse flow of university lectures to see how frequently the different functions occur within the structure of discourse.

These approaches to studying language use in registers provide detailed analyses of these individual features and their individual patterns. Therefore, we can learn a good deal about the use of that one feature. While these studies are interesting and very informative for these features separately, as Csomay indicates, "comprehensive descriptions of variation in language use cannot be based on investigating a single linguistic form or a single linguistic feature in isolation" (2015: 5). When describing the linguistic characteristics of texts, relying on one feature at a time is difficult mostly because a) an *a priori* selection of that one feature is hard to predict, since we would not really know which feature will mark the difference in the situations we are comparing, and because, as mentioned above, b) language features are typically in relationship with each other and do not occur in a vacuum. In order to characterize a register, we would need to provide a comprehensive analysis. For a comprehensive analysis, we need to look at all linguistic features in texts. In addition, we need to examine their distributional patterns to gain a "full" picture as to what linguistic features registers may be made up of. While this is possible, we would still lack the understanding of how various language features relate to one another.

However, as mentioned above, in this book, we will mainly focus on individual linguistic features and their variation in registers for two main reasons. On the one hand, these kinds of studies are relatively easy to carry out without the necessary background knowledge for a more sophisticated type of study. On the other hand, and tied to the previous point, our book is for a relatively novice audience. It is written for someone doing corpus linguistics perhaps even for the first time and for someone who has limited or no basic statistical knowledge. In contrast, to carry out comprehensive linguistic analyses from the start, the researcher must have a solid background in computer programming and in multivariate statistical methods. While such methodology is not the focus of this book, based on the results of previous comprehensive studies, we will point to ways a cluster of already identified features could be analyzed and discuss how they could be useful for our own analyses.

2.6 End of Chapter Exercises

1. In this chapter, we have discussed some benefits of investigating language from a register-functional perspective. In your opinion, what is the advantage of register variation in corpus linguistics as opposed to other possibilities, such as genre analysis or analysis of style? What types of linguistic methods are suited to genre or style analysis?

2. Go to COCA and pick two subcategories. Line up the situational characteristics for each, the way it is done in this chapter, to see what the differences are.

3. Relationship between sociolinguistics and register variation: Given what you know about traditional sociolinguistic variation, which of the seven situational factors described in Figure 2.1 would you attribute to traditional sociolinguistic factors?

4. Look back on the situational analysis presented in 2.3.1 and think about what linguistic features are worthy of closer investigation. Before you focus on one or two features for comparison, look at the text in Table 2.6 and identify features found in one text but not in the other.

Table 2.6 Texts from an email to a friend and an email to a boss

Email to a friend	Email to a boss
hey! guess what? today leah announced she had a present for me and handed me a Marriott card that said "tad cross" and i said "WTF?" and she informed me that our colleague flora had met him at a conference, one in which he played a leading role, and he'd mentioned my name. this evening in the parking lot she told me, "he's VERY handsome." flora's 65 and likely thinks everyone's handsome, but i had to admit i'd had a huge crush on him when i was a wee one. haven't seen him since, but i'd love a reminder on what he's up to. i seem to remember something funny (uber christian?), but also that lynn loves him. and i plan to attend that conference next year, so eventually i might find out for meself.	Hello __, As I may have mentioned to you before, I'm currently taking a Ph. D seminar in speech perception, and Dr. ___ ___ has been guiding all of us towards conducting some sort of research project this semester. The project I have chosen relates to teaching pronunciation skills in a reading classroom, and whether or not this (constituting a brief and non-interfering classroom treatment) will improve students reading fluency and receptive vocabulary (as reflected in the week 1 assessment). If you're willing, I'd like to meet with you at your earliest convenience, so that I can ask you a couple of questions regarding this. I would like to work with level 3 students if possible, which I believe you coordinate (for reading and writing class). I have cc'd Dr. ___ on this email, as per what I am told is the policy for discussing potential research in classes. Please let me know when and if you have some free time to talk.

Notes

1 Since these text segments are uneven in length (one is 157 words long and the other is 241 words long), we had to scale the raw frequency counts as if both texts were 100 words long. To do this, we need to norm the feature count with a simple statistic: (raw feature count / actual text length) * desired text length. We will discuss this technique more in subsequent chapters.

2 To calculate type-token ratios, we take the number of words in a text and divide it by the number of word types. If a word is repeated, it counts as a new token but not as a new type. For example, in the following two sentences, there are ten tokens (i.e., number of words) and eight types (because "the" and "cat" are repeated): *He saw the cat. The cat was in the garage.*

References

Biber, D. (1988). *Variation across speech and writing*. Cambridge University Press.

Biber, D., & Conrad, S. (2019). *Register, genre and style* (2nd ed.). Cambridge University Press.

Biber, D., Conrad, S., Reppen, R., Byrd, P., & Helt, M. (2002). Speaking and writing in the university: A multidimensional comparison. *TESOL Quarterly, 36*, 9–48.

Biber, D., Conrad, S., & Cortes, V. (2004). "If you look at …": Lexical Bundles in university teaching and textbooks. *Applied Linguistics, 25*(3), 371–405.

Biber, D., Gray, B., Staples, S., & Egbert, J. (2022). *The register-functional approach to grammatical complexity: Theoretical foundation, descriptive research findings, application*. Routledge.

Biber, D., Johansson, S., Leech, G., Conrad, S., & Finegan, E. (1999). *Longman grammar of spoken and written English*. Longman.

Csomay, E. (2013). Lexical bundles in discourse structure: A corpus-based study of classroom discourse. *Applied Linguistics, 34*, 369–388.

Csomay, E. (2015). A corpus-based analysis of linguistic variation in teacher and student presentations in university settings. In V. Cortes & E. Csomay (Eds.), *Corpus-based research in applied linguistics. Studies in honor of Doug Biber* (pp. 1–23). John Benjamins.

Duranti, A. (1985). Sociocultural dimensions of discourse. In Teun van Dijk (Ed.), *Handbook of discourse analysis* (pp. 193–230). Academic Press.

Fortanet, I. (2004). The use of "we" in university lectures: Reference and function. *English for Specific Purposes, 23*, 45–66.

Halliday, M. A. K. (1978). *Language as social semiotic: The social interpretation of language and meaning*. Edward Arnold.

Hymes, D. (1974). *Foundations of sociolinguistics: An ethnographic approach*. University of Pennsylvania Press.

Wulff, S., Römer, U., & Swales, J. (2012). Attended/unattended *this* in academic student writing: Quantitative and qualitative perspectives. In E. Csomay (Ed.), *Contemporary perspectives on discourse and corpora*. Special issue of *Corpus Linguistics and Linguistic Theory*, (8)1, 129–157.

Part II

Searches in Available Corpora

Chapter 3

Searching a Corpus

When researchers use corpora for their analyses, they are interested in exploring the use of lexical items, or certain grammatical constructions. They may also investigate lexical or grammatical patterns to see how variation in those patterns may relate to different contexts. In register studies, as we saw in the previous chapters, contextual differences refer to differences in particular aspects of the situational characteristics in the construction and production of a given text.

In this chapter, we will use the Corpus of Contemporary American English (COCA) to illustrate the most commonly identified units of language that researchers use for their analyses: words, collocations, n-grams/lexical bundles for lexical patterns, and part of speech (POS) tags for grammatical patterns. We will illustrate how to identify these units of language by providing different tasks that will give you practice in searching and analyzing these units of language. In addition, we will suggest that you access other corpora to carry out further projects in this area, for example, the Michigan Corpus of Academic Spoken English (MICASE). We will also recommend a software tool, AntConc, to carry out a keyword analysis (further details on the software is in Chapter 5). This chapter is divided into four main sections: 1) Words with two subsections: KWIC (keyword in context) and keyword analysis (based on word frequency); 2) Collocations; 3) N-grams; 4) POS tags.

Before we can start, you will need to do two things: 1) register with COCA as a student, so you can have extended searches in that database and 2) download the latest version of AntConc (currently 4.2.0), so you

DOI: 10.4324/9781003363309-5

can run that program for your keyword analysis. Both COCA and Ant-Conc are free of charge.

To register with COCA, go to COCA (www.english-corpora.org/coca/) and, on the top right, click on the icon with a person's head in a box (marked yellow) and then click on "Register". This site will periodically ask you to donate money; however, as we mentioned in the previous chapter, it is not a requirement for your registration. Once you sign in, the icon with the figurehead turns green instead of yellow.

To access MICASE you can go to the address below. It is free with no sign-up, but they do ask that you make appropriate references when you carry out research with the texts available through that corpus (https://quod.lib.umich.edu/cgi/c/corpus/corpus?c=micase;page=simple).

To download AntConc, go to Laurence Anthony's software page, and download the latest version (currently 4.2.0) to your system (Mac, Windows, or Linux) knowing that we are using the Windows version in our discussions (https://www.laurenceanthony.net/software/antconc/). (See our discussion on AntConc further in Chapter 5.)

3.1 Words

3.1.1 Keyword in Context (KWIC)

Let's say that we are interested in searching COCA to see how often the word "say" is used across three registers: spoken discourse, newspaper, and academic prose. As we described in the previous chapter, after logging into the latest version of COCA (currently 2023), you have different choices, namely, choose "list", which will provide you with concordance lines, "chart" which will provide a chart of the frequency of your selected keyword in different registers, or "word" which will give you a plethora of information about the word you are searching (e.g., collocations, synonyms, clusters, related words, and much more). Try your hand with the different options by looking up any keyword you wish so you can see what kinds of information is available to you!

The keyword that we are searching for here and now is "say". If you click on "chart", you get a summary of the frequency distribution for this word across registers. As we see on the chart in Figure 3.1 (on the left-hand side in the figure under "ALL"), our keyword occurs a total of 968,328 times in the entire corpus; that is, on average 975.13[1] times per million words, including all the registers in the corpus.[2] We can also see the distributional patterns across the registers. Our interest is in three registers: spoken, newspaper, and academic prose. It is apparent, perhaps not surprisingly, that our keyword occurs, on average, most often in spoken discourse (1,937.05 times in a million words) under "SPOKEN", followed by newspapers (831.94) under "NEWSPAPER", and finally academic prose (216.88) as shown under "ACADEMIC". We note that two other registers, TV shows/movies and fiction, also have a high frequency for this word but for our analysis here, we are interested in the three registers mentioned above, namely, spoken, newspaper, and academic. Since we have not yet specified what part of speech we are looking at, and "say" can be both a verb (he *said* he was going to be late) and a noun (he has the final *say* in the matter), these numbers include all of these options.

If we were interested in how our keyword is used in the immediate textual context, we would select "context" from the choices on top as shown in Figure 3.1 to get to the window shown in Figure 3.2. Now, as you see, our keyword is not just an individual word but it is placed back into its textual environment. The program randomly selects examples from the corpus and lists each occurrence of our keyword together with a window of text around it. This kind of listing is called "concordance lines".

When we use concordance lines, we look for individual (or a group of) pre-selected keywords to see them in their immediate context. The most common form to display a keyword in context (KWIC) is through concordance lines. As mentioned above, concordance lines highlight the word you pick and provide additional text around it. You can set the size of the text by selecting the number of characters (see our discussion on AntConc in Chapter 5) in the window around the keyword, and the output lists the examples selected from the text. Each time you run the search, even with the same keyword (by choosing the button "KWIC" in the top left corner of COCA), it will display a different set of randomly selected examples.

Why would the textual environment be interesting? Because you can see the word in context now, you will be able to see patterns surrounding the

SECTION	ALL	BLOG	WEB	TV/M	SPOK	FIC	MAG	NEWS	ACAD	1990-94	1995-99	2000-04	2005-09	2010-14	2015-19
FREQ	968328	116076	103042	191882	244331	113834	71901	101292	25080	124927	130628	128076	123498	122530	119551
WORDS (M)	993	128.6	124.3	128.1	126.1	118.3	120.1	121.7	113.8	121.1	125.2	124.6	123.1	123.3	122.8
PER MIL	975.13	902.52	829.29	1,498.21	1,937.05	962.07	570.23	831.94	216.88	1,031.54	1,043.27	1,027.70	1,003.43	993.37	973.92

Figure 3.1 Distributional patterns of the word "say" in COCA

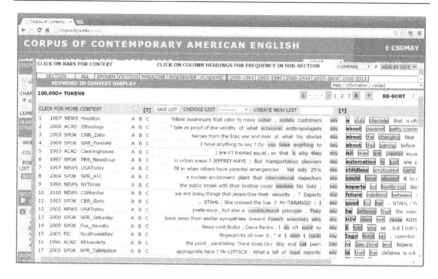

Figure 3.2 Concordance lines for the word "say" in COCA

word. Let's see what kinds of words follow our keyword. More specifically, let's see what part of speech categories seem to be following our keyword.

When you access COCA, the different colors denote different part of speech categories (here everything is black and white only). You can get the full list of what the colors mean via the website, but for now, let's pick a few: verbs are pink, prepositions, as in "say *in* the paper", are marked as yellow; nouns are turquoise, as in "I heard him say *abstinence*"; and adverbs and adverbials are in orange, as in "They all say *basically* the same".

Project 3.1: "Say" Followed by What Part of Speech?

Given the 100 randomly selected examples that you see, answer the research question "What is the distribution of the different part of speech categories following the keyword 'say' when it is a verb?". To answer this question, create a table (see Table 3.1 as an example) and enter how many nouns, pronouns, adjectives, "that" complementizers, or punctuation marks you see (each will be a different color) following the verb "say". (Reminder: The keyword "say" must be a verb, hence, marked pink.) Can you state some general patterns that you see in the dataset based on these examples?

Table 3.1 Distribution of part of speech categories following the word "say"

"SAY"	NOUN	PRONOUN	ADJECTIVE	PUNCTUATION	"THAT"	OTHER	Total
							100

Project 3.2: "Say", POS, and Register

For this project, your new research questions are: "What is the distribution of the different part of speech categories following the keyword 'say' (when it is a verb) in spoken discourse versus academic prose?" and "Is there a difference in use?"

In this case, since you are more interested in how your keyword is used in different registers, you would want 100 sample concordance lines randomly selected from spoken discourse, and 100 concordance lines randomly selected from academic prose. To get those concordance lines for your sample, go to the main page of COCA, click on "chart" and type in "sa*_v" in the search box. This will select only instances of "say" as a verb and show you the distributional pattern across several registers. Click on the bar for spoken discourse (SPOK) and that will give you 100 sample cases when the verb "say" occurs in spoken discourse. Type in "say_spoken" under "Create new list" above the sample concordance lines and save the list. Then click on the academic prose bar to get your second 100 samples just from that register; save it as "say_academic". Create a table like Table 3.2. Based on your results, what can you tell us about how these two registers use "say" in terms of their syntactic environment?

Project 3.3: "Say" and "State"

You also know that "say" and "state" are synonyms, so they could be used interchangeably when they are verbs – at least in terms of syntax and semantics. For simplicity, let's just pick the past tense/participle forms of these two verbs: "stated" and "said". You may predict that different registers probably use these two verbs differently because one is considered more "formal" than the other. Your research question is: "What is the frequency and distributional pattern of 'say' and 'state' (as verbs in past tense and participial forms) in three registers: spoken discourse, newspaper, and academic prose?" Create a table suggested in Table 3.3 to present your results. Can you see any patterns you can report on?

Table 3.2 Distribution of part of speech categories following the word "say" in spoken discourse and in academic prose

"SAY"	NOUN	PRONOUN	ADJECTIVE	PUNCTUATION	"THAT"	OTHER	Total
Spoken							100
Acad. Prose							100

Table 3.3 Raw and normed frequency counts for "said" and "stated" in three registers

	SAY/SAID		STATE/STATED	
	Raw frequency	Normed frequency to 1 million words	Raw frequency	Normed frequency to 1 million words
Spoken				
Newspaper				
Academic Prose				

Project 3.4: "Said" and "Stated"

Now, have a closer look at the environment to see how these forms are actually used. Take a sample of 100 randomly selected sentences from spoken and another 100 from academic prose for each of the two words (you will have a total of 400 sentences, 200 for "said" and 200 for "stated") and categorize the functions of the past tense/participle forms, trying to answer the following research question: "What is the distributional pattern for the following functions?":

- To state an action in the past, as in "She *said* that he had gone to the party"
- To state a completed action with a result relevant in the present (present perfect), as in "He has *stated* his rights already"
- To state action completed in the past prior to a past action (past perfect), as in "I had *said* that before"
- To modify a noun (adjectival function), as in "the *stated* example"?

Fill in Table 3.4 below with your numbers. Are there any differences in the functions across registers?

Table 3.4 Distribution of "said" and "stated" in two registers

	Past action	Perfect aspect	Past perfect	Adjectival	Other	Total
SAID spoken						100
SAID academic						100
STATED spoken						100
STATED academic						100

3.1.2 Keyword Analysis

Through a keyword analysis, you can identify words that exist in one text but not in another text. In other words, a keyword analysis helps you identify unique words in a text (keywords) when you compare that text with another text. You can also compare two corpora that are made up of several texts. In this case, you compare words in one corpus, called target corpus, with words in another, called reference corpus.

Keyness defined this way was first promoted by Williams (1986), who believed that words that are key "capture the essence of particular social, cultural or political themes, thoughts or discourses" (Culpeper & Demmen, 2015: 90). Other scholars think about keywords somewhat differently and say that keywords a) represent the "aboutness" of a text (Scott, 1997), b) reflect stylistic features when examined in context (Scott & Tribble, 2006), or c) show "the communicative purpose and micro- or macrostructure of the text" (Bondi, 2010: 7) where "some words seem more central to the text than others (Phillips, 1985)" (Csomay & Young, 2021: 75). In a keyword analysis, the frequency counts of every word in a text or in a corpus as a whole is compared to its frequency in the reference text, or reference corpus (Scott & Tribble, 2006).

We list a few studies next where scholars have used keyword analysis, so you can have an idea of what kinds of questions they were interested in:

1. Words used by different characters in classic literary works have been a very popular topic for keyword analyses. For example, Culpeper (2009) analyzed characters in Shakespearean drama. More specifically, he compared words uttered by different characters in *Romeo and Juliet* and concluded that the words characters use differ a great deal, and, indeed, reflect their state of mind and their character. Fischer-Starcke (2009) investigated *Pride and Prejudice* written by Jane Austen and claimed that with a quantitative approach to text analysis, i.e., keyword analysis, we are able to uncover meanings that literary analyses are unable to uncover and that is due to the different methodology, such as keyword analysis, applied.

2. With the same goal of identifying words used by specific characters, Bednarek (2010) focused on telecinematic discourse. She studied different characters in *Gilmore Girls* and showed that "keywords relate to character aspects such as their age, environment and relationships, and can provide insights into characters' unique voices" (Csomay & Young, 2021: 74). Another study by Bednarek (2011) reported on specific aspects of character identity (e.g., nerdiness) or the stability of one specific character, Lorelai, in *Gilmore Girls* over the course of its seven seasons in her corpus and via a keyword analysis.

3. Another example of tracking keywords in telecinematic discourse leads to conclusions about changing gender roles through time. This work is exemplified by Csomay and Young (2021) as they compared vocabulary use by male and female characters in three seasons of *Star Trek* episodes spanning several years and multiple decades (1966–1969; 1987–1994; 1993–1997). Through a keyword analysis comparing male and female use of vocabulary through the three different time periods, they found significant differences in vocabulary use that clearly reflected changes in gender roles in society through time.

With these studies in mind, the next project will compare two corpora already available through AntConc. Let's say, we are interested in finding out how American press reporting is different from British press reports in terms of vocabulary. You probably know the answer already that there are many words that would be different, but this project will look for some specific examples to show how you can support a perspective with empirical data. Our research question is: "How does vocabulary in American press reporting differ from words used in British press reporting?"

Before we start, please watch the tutorial on how to use the keyword feature in AntConc: www.youtube.com/watch?v=SludW4FHatI&list=PLiRIDpYmiC0SjJeT2FuysOkLa45HG_tIu&index=10. Since we are using already existing corpora in AntConc, there is no need to upload any texts from your own corpus, but as the tutorial says, you are more than welcome to do that as well for other projects (including the related projects described below).

Step 1. Following the online tutorial on YouTube referenced above, identify the press reports sub-corpus in both the American and the British collections (AmE06_PressRep and BE-06_PressRep) and feed them into the tool. The British press reporting is your target corpus and the American press reporting is your reference corpus.

a) Go to File → Open corpus manager
b) Download the required sub-corpora into the program; you have successfully downloaded the texts if the little diamond shape becomes green
c) Highlight the British press reporting text (the line becomes blue) and press "choose", making sure that the tab on the right-hand window is on "target corpus"; then repeat the same for the American press reporting but now your tab will be on "reference corpus".

Step 2. Once you have downloaded the appropriate sub-corpora, run the analysis by clicking on the "start" button.

Figure 3.3 shows what your window should look like.

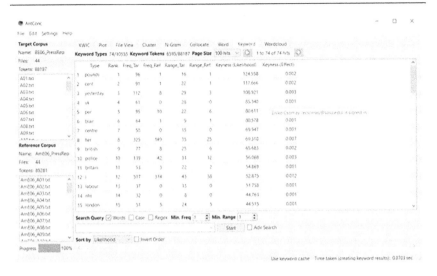

Figure 3.3 Results from the keyword analysis for British and American press reporting

The higher the keyness value for the words, the more likely that they appear in the target versus the reference corpus. The words in Figure 3.3 are ranked based on their keyness value. As you see from the results in Figure 3.3, there are 76 words that are more likely to appear in the target corpus compared to the reference corpus. As you can see, the word "pound" has the highest keyness value. This is not surprising, since our target corpus has 44 texts of British press reporting. However, the word "pound" could refer to two things: the British pound (a monetary measure) or lbs (a weight measure). If you click on the word in the result window, you will see several examples of how the word is used in context (KWIC). In this case, as the examples show, "pound" is clearly used as a monetary measure, e.g., "… ordered to hand back almost a quarter of a million pounds, say the police …". It is clear that this word is more likely to appear in the target corpus than in American press reports, which is the reference corpus. In fact, further data shows that the word "pound" appeared 96 times in the British press corpus and one time in the American press corpus, and that those 96 occurrences appeared in 16 files out of a total of 44.

Another example is the word "blair" ranked as sixth on the list. This word clearly refers to Tony Blair, a former Prime Minister of Great Britain, and will be more prominent in British than in American press reporting (64 times in nine texts versus one time in one text, respectively).

Project 3.5: Keywords in British versus American Press Reporting

After running the texts as described above, what other words can you identify on the list that are clearly more likely to be used in the British press? For example, UK, Britain, London ... Can you group them based on some category that is contextually driven (like the analysis above may suggest)? For example, references to Great Britain as a context (its institutions, cities, etc.). Can you think of any other groupings that you could come up with? (Hint: Do you see anything that may be special from a linguistic point of view?)

Project 3.6: Context-Specific Terms

Click twice on the word "nhs". Do you know what it means? Do you think it is an acronym? What makes you think so? What do you notice about this word in terms of its spelling? Can you guess from the context what it may stand for? If not, look it up on Google.

Now click twice on the word "labour". Let's predict why this word is more likely to be used in British over American press reportage. What is the meaning/synonym of "labour"? Yes, it has something to do with work. Click on the word twice to see how it is used in context. What do you notice? Read some of the concordance lines and try to answer the question: Why do you think it is used with a capital "L"?

Project 3.7: Keywords in Your Corpora

If you want to work with your own texts, for example, from the Michigan Corpus of Academic Spoken Discourse (MICASE), you will need to download the texts first, save them as text files, and then feed them into AntConc (see YouTube tutorial).

If you need to convert webtext, i.e., from html to text, follow the steps on this website: www.computerhope.com/issues/ch001877.htm#text. If you need to convert pdf files to a text format, the best tool to use is another free program by Laurence Anthony, and it is called AntFileConverter: www.laurenceanthony.net/software/antfileconverter/. Once you have your texts in .txt format, you can go back to the tutorial and learn how to feed them into the AntConc program.

The one thing to keep in mind when you compare corpora for a keyword analysis is to choose corpora that are approximately the same size in terms of the number of words in them. A corpus with more or longer texts will allow more words in them. With more words, the frequency of each word increases and since the keyword analysis is based on frequency in one corpus over another (see tutorial), this may be problematic if you have different-sized corpora.

If you use MICASE, you can compare two different disciplinary areas to see whether they use certain words in one discipline versus another. To do so, select two disciplinary areas you are interested in – for us, it is history and natural sciences (natural resources). If you select these areas, you will be given multiple texts to choose from. Select the file titled "History Review Discussion Section" (DIS315JU101) and "Ecological Agriculture Colloquium" (COL 425MX075). We will use two areas because they have about the same number of words in the files. Download the files and make sure they are saved in text format (see the website referenced above on how to do that). Run the keyword analysis and then determine what sort of groupings you can identify for the types of words one session is using over the other.

3.2 Collocates

As mentioned in Chapter 1, collocates are two words that occur together more often than we would expect by chance. More specifically, Webster's dictionary defines *collocate* as a word that is "habitually juxtaposed with another with a frequency greater than chance". Firth (1951) coined the term "collocation" to refer to two words that go together. Some words, even though they may mean roughly the same thing, may not go together. In the following example, in each instance, we want to express the fact that something went bad. However, while we often say *rancid butter*, we rarely, if at all, say **sour butter*, and, in fact, that sounds odd to some people. The latter two words do not seem to go together in English. The same is true for *sour milk*, which is a collocate, while **rancid milk* might sound odd. Another example could be *strong tea* versus **powerful tea* and *powerful computers* versus **strong computers*. There are many further examples of two words going together. These could be partially or fully fixed expressions and they are used in particular contexts. Although these examples show adjective + noun combinations only, it is not the case that only these two parts of speech categories go together. Other collocate types are, for example, noun + noun (e.g., *bus stop*) combinations, verb + noun (e.g., *spend money*), verb + prepositional phrase (e.g., *account for*), and so on.

Project 3.8: Collocates of "Spend"

Go to the main page of COCA, type in "spend", and click on "Word" among the list of options. On this page, you have all kinds of information about the word spend, including what words they collocate with. Look at what collocates this word has. You will see that the collocates are, for example, *spend time, money, day*, etc. If you click on the word "time" from this collocate listing and scroll down, you will be able to bring up all the examples where these two words occur together in texts. Click on "money", and examine the first 100 samples provided to you, answering the following research question: "In which register does the collocate *spend* (v) + *time* occur most frequently (in your sample)?" Another way of looking at collocates is if you click on the link called "Collocates" in the top right, you will see all the collocates with the word "spend" and for each, you can see their frequency counts as well.

3.3 N-Grams

Most often, n-grams in linguistics are sequences of words explored as a unit, where the value of *n* denotes how many words there are in that unit. If the basic unit of analysis is a word, then we can call that a uni-gram (1-gram). If we have two words to consider as a unit, they are bi-grams (2-grams), and if we have three words as a sequence in a unit, it will be a tri-gram (3-gram), and so on.

A special computer program is often designed to process the text and to look at sequences of words in a window of text as they emerge in a corpus. Depending on how "big" your unit is (i.e., how many words in a sequence you want to trace at a given point in time), the window size is set accordingly. That is, if you want to identify bi-grams, you will capture each two-word sequence in the corpus. If you are looking for tri-grams, you will capture each three-word sequence, and so on. As you are doing so, the already identified sequences are tracked and the new sequences are constantly checked against what the program has already found. Each time the same word sequence is found, the program counts the frequencies of that sequence. We can explore how frequently particular word combinations (n-grams) occur together in a corpus or how they are distributed across different registers.

If you know ahead of time what sequences you are looking for, you can just type the sequence in the search engine. In this case, you are not looking for the kinds of n-grams that may be emerging in that corpus; instead, you are just looking for a pre-defined sequence of words (that may, or may not, have been extracted from a previous corpus). For example, if you type in the word *baby*, you will see that it occurs over 60,000 times in the COCA corpus. But you picked the word ahead of time, so you knew what to look for. If you are interested in the sequence *a baby*, it occurs more than 10,000 times in the same corpus, and if you are interested in the sequence *like a baby*, you will see that it occurs more than 600 times in COCA. At the same time, the four-word sequence *sleep like a baby* only appears 25 times in the same corpus. In all of these instances, however, you have typed in the words that you were interested in.

In contrast, if you don't know what you want to look for ahead of time, but you are interested in the possibilities a corpus may have, you can either design a new computer program for yourself and run your own data, or run the n-gram program already available to you (e.g., through AntConc, a software that we discuss more in Chapter 5). The COCA site actually provides the lists for you, including bi-, tri-, four-, and five-grams, and their frequencies in COCA.

3.3.1 One-Grams or Uni-Grams and Individual Words

When you search for uni-grams, you are basically interested in individual words. When you know ahead of time what word you are interested in, they are often referred to as "keywords". As we have discussed earlier in this chapter, in the KWIC section, you could then see your keyword in a textual context. The purpose of your search for keywords could be that you analyze a) what kinds of words surround your keyword, b) how they are positioned in the sentence or in the phrase, or c) what the frequencies are of your keywords. We have illustrated how this may work in the previous chapter.

Project 3.9: "WAY"

Go to COCA and search for the word (or 1-gram) *way*. Click on the chart button. Report on the overall frequency of the keyword "way", its normed frequency, and its distributional patterns across all seven registers (as well as their use through time) noted in COCA – namely, spoken discourse, fiction, magazine, TV shows and movies, newspaper, and academic prose.

Project 3.10: Frequency Rank of "A" Versus "Juxtaposition"

Let's have a look at the vocabulary characteristics of a text. This way we can investigate patterns in larger units such as a text. Each word in the COCA corpus is classified into frequency bands. That is, each word is ranked depending on how often it occurs in COCA. For example, the third person pronoun *he* is ranked as the 15th most frequently occurring word in the corpus with a frequency of 6,468,335. The word *way*, when a noun is ranked 82nd in COCA with a total frequency of 1,260,011. The most frequently occurring words in general are function words – for example, articles (*a*, *an*, and *the*) or prepositions or particles (*in*, *on*, etc.). In fact, the definite article *the* is ranked #1 in the corpus with a frequency of 50,017,617. Now compare the rank and frequency of the word *juxtaposition* (as a noun) to the indefinite article that you have just searched. What is the rank and what is the frequency for this word? Is it a frequent word in the corpus?

Project 3.11: Vocabulary Characteristics of a Text

Go to COCA's main page and click on the icon that looks like a page of writing or a page of typed text (Figure 3.4).

Now, as we mentioned above, we can explore how many very frequent or less frequent words are used in a text. From the "Samples" drop-down menu on the top left-hand side, pick FICTION. A random sample text from the fiction sub-corpus will appear in the text box that will then be analyzed for its vocabulary make-up. In this case, we get a sample from *Literary Review: The Search for the Gold Finger.* Click on "Analyze text". On the left-hand side, you will find the same text but now marked up with different colors. The color each word gets will depend on where the word ranks as a frequently occurring word in the database. (See Figure 3.5.)

As you see, there are three frequency bands. Words marked with the color blue are among the top 500 most frequently occurring words in the corpus. The green ones rank as the top 501–3,000 most frequently occurring words in the corpus, and the yellow ones are marked for those that are in the rank of less commonly used vocabulary in the corpus (beyond the rank of 3,000). Be careful not to interpret these as frequencies because these are rank numbers. You can see the actual words from the text in these three bands on the right-hand side. Their frequency in that text is also shown. For example, the word "thief" is a low-frequency word (in band three marked with yellow) and it occurs three times in this text. If we jump to the frequency band, we see that the word "the" occurs 22 times in this text sample.

While Figure 3.5 is black and white only, if you go to the COCA site and follow the steps above, you will see the colors. Nonetheless, in the text in Figure 3.5, there are a lot of blue words indicating that many of the vocabulary items in this text are taken from the first band. These are words that ranked high based on their frequency in COCA. The text shown in Figure 3.5 contains a lot of frequently occurring vocabulary and a relatively small number of words occurring less frequently in COCA (marked in yellow). In fact, as you may also notice, for each frequency band, the percentage of the vocabulary items for that band in the text is indicated. In the example in Figure 3.5, the text was randomly chosen by the program as we clicked on fiction. The text has the following vocabulary characteristics:

Figure 3.4 Icons on the top to choose from for the next project

a total of 404 words, of which 58% are words that fall in to the first frequency band. That is, 58% of the words in this text are among the most frequent words in the corpus that ranked among the first 500 most frequently occurring words. In addition, 12% of the words fall in the second band, and 10% fall in the third band.

If you click on any of the words in the list, it gives you information about that one word in terms of its distributional patterns across the different registers, provides a definition of the word and its collocates, and also provides examples from the COCA corpus in concordance lines. For example, if you select "thief", you will see the window shown in Figure 3.6.

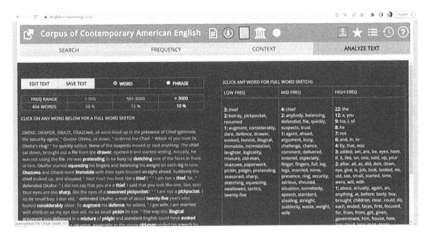

Figure 3.5 Text analysis based on vocabulary frequency in Word and Phrase

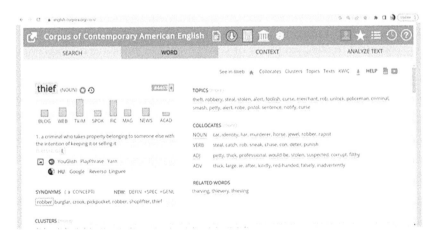

Figure 3.6 More information about the word "thief"

If you scroll down the same screen, you are able to see the concordance lines generated from COCA on the word "thief" (Figure 3.7) as the keyword in context (KWIC).

Figure 3.7 Concordance lines for the word "thief"

Project 3.12: Vocabulary and Academic Prose

In our example above, we used a sample from fiction as a register and looked at different kinds of words in the text. Following the same steps outlined above, choose a sample from another register – for example, academic prose (marked as ACADEMIC on the list). Follow the same steps to look at how many and what kinds of words you see in this text sample. Do you see any difference between the two registers in terms of the percentage of frequent (or not frequent) words in the text? Report your results.

If you want to check any text of your choice, all you have to do is copy and paste the text in the textbox and the words will be marked up for your text in the same way as it is done in the examples. The frequencies, once again, were identified in COCA. It is a great baseline corpus for your own research as well. This is a very powerful and useful tool to determine the vocabulary characteristics of a text. Can you think of ways you may be able to use this tool for your own writing?

3.3.2 Bi-Grams and Collocates

Bi-grams are two words in sequence. The difference between bi-grams and collocations is the fact that bi-grams are identified based on two words that happen to be next to each other in a corpus while collocations are two words co-occurring more frequently than by chance. Collocates are always two-word combinations, are statistically determined, and are also called 2-grams (or bi-grams), as mentioned before. All collocates are bi-grams but not all bi-grams are collocates.

Project 3.13: "Way" and Its Collocates

Look for the prepositions that are found with the word *way*. In COCA, type in *way*, click on "collocates" and type in the following: [[way]]. [nn*] * [i*]. This string indicates that we are looking for the word *way* as a noun, and we are looking for prepositions that follow it whether immediately after the word or within a window of text to the right up to four words. The results will look like in Figure 3.8.

As part of your qualitative analysis, you may want to see some of the meaning differences when you use different types of prepositions, or how a second particle or preposition is attached.

3.3.3 Tri-Grams

Any three words co-occurring together in the same sequence are known as tri-grams. Some are complete structural or semantic units such as *by the way* or *in a way*, and can be treated as fixed expressions with a specific meaning. Others may be a semi-structural unit such as *by way of*, which is

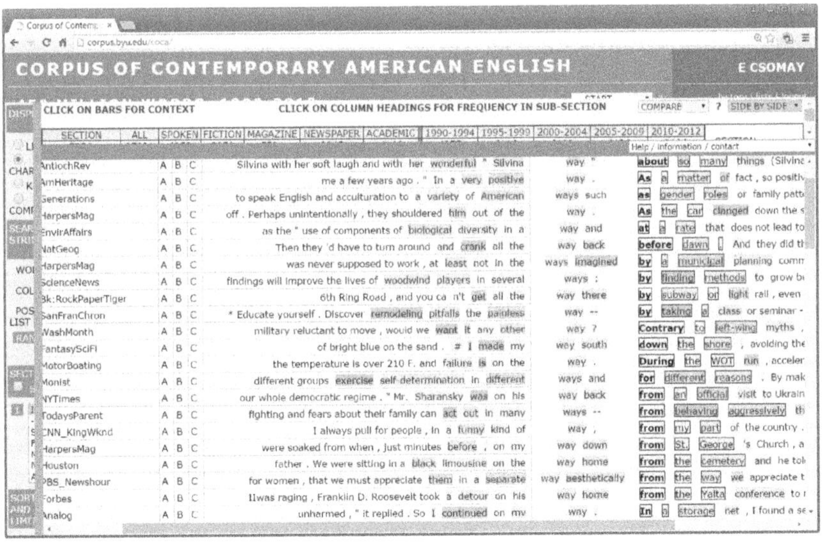

Figure 3.8 Part of speech search in COCA

missing one element coming after it in the phrase, or have a gap in meaning such as *what would you*. Most recent studies have explored the possibilities of what could potentially come before or after a tri-gram in terms of their structural correlates (Cortes, 2014).

Project 3.14: "By the Way" in Registers

Let's look at COCA again. It is a common belief that *by the way* is used only in spoken discourse, and never in academic prose. First, let's search for *by the way* in two registers: spoken and academic prose. Make a frequency table as we did before and report on their distributional patterns. Do you see anything interesting to report or discuss?

Project 3.15: "By the Way" and "In a Way"

It is believed that both *by the way* and *in a way* are used as sentence adverbials. Make a general search for each and see whether this could be supported by the 100 examples that you have found. Another aspect of this would be to look at where these tri-grams appear in a sentence or utterance. Look at your 100-item sample in each of the two registers and determine whether they are always at the beginning of a sentence or utterance. Is there a difference between the two registers from this perspective?

Project 3.16: "By Way of" What?

Type *by way of* into the top and the command [nn*]. This string *by way of [nn*]* will allow you to search for nouns that come after the tri-gram *by way of*. This command will give you the strings and will list the nouns following the string.

Step 1: Click on "chart" and the button below where you typed in your string above. This will give you the distributional patterns of this construction (with any nouns) following the tri-gram. Then click on the SPOK (spoken discourse) bar. This will provide you with examples from spoken discourse. Once you have 100 randomly selected samples, classify the nouns into semantic categories (you may want to go to Biber et al.'s [1999] *Longman Grammar of English* or some other descriptive grammar of English for examples of semantic categories of nouns).

Step 2: Follow the same procedures as in Step 1 but now select ACAD (academic discourse) to get examples from that register. Classify the nouns into semantic categories.

Is there a difference between spoken and academic discourse in the kinds of nouns that are used after *by way of*?

When tri-grams occur with a particular frequency (e.g., 20 times) and in one specific register in a corpus, they are often called lexical bundles. However, four-grams are most generally investigated as lexical bundles and are discussed in the following section.

3.3.4 Four-Grams and Lexical Bundles

Four-grams are sequences of four words occurring together in a corpus. When we call them 4-grams, it does not matter how often they occur in a corpus; they are still called 4-grams. That is, every four-word sequence in a corpus is a 4-gram. However, similar to tri-grams, when these four-word combinations occur at least 10 or 20 or more times in a million words (depending on how conservative we want to be) and appear in at least five different texts (to avoid idiosyncratic – that is, individualistic – use) in a register, they are referred to as "lexical bundles" in the literature (see the background on lexical bundles in Cortes, 2015). Lexical bundles were first identified and named by Biber and Conrad in 1999, and were described in detail by Biber et al. (1999). Since then, many studies have reported on various aspects of these bundles. For example, even though they are not always complete structural or semantic units, scholars have described them for their structural and functional make-up. They have been investigated in a broad number of registers (Biber et al., 2004) and in specific registers such as university language (Biber & Barbieri, 2007). Most recently, they were also examined for their position in the structure of discourse (Cso-may, 2013) to see relationships between their functions and their position in texts. Other studies go inside the bundles to see which elements in the bundles are more "fixed" than others (Biber, 2009) or they look at what kind of semantic categorization can be done on the words immediately sur-rounding the actual bundle (e.g., Cortes, 2014).

Lexical bundles, a special type of four-word sequences, are defined by the number of times they occur in a million words in a register. As men-tioned above, they are not necessarily structurally complete units, e.g., *in the case of*. But sometimes, they happen to be units that we recognize and know quite well, such as *if you look at* in classroom discourse or *on the other hand* in academic prose. The latter is a semantically and functionally complete unit even though that is not a typical characteristic of bundles by definition, and, therefore, it is not common to find these among bundles. Given that earlier studies (especially Biber et al., 2004) classified these four-word sequences, or lexical bundles, based on their grammatical as well as functional categories, we can add to our understanding of how lexical bun-dles are used if we investigated where in the sentence the lexical bundles are positioned and whether there is a difference in the distribution of those positions in, let's say, written and spoken registers. Shall we find out?

Project 3.17: "On the Other Hand"

Go to COCA, sign in, and type in *on the other hand*. Hit "chart" and then the search button below the area where you typed in your expression. You should be able to see something like Figure 3.9.

Report on what you see in terms of spoken/academic usage of the lexical bundle *on the other hand* in the COCA corpus. Then click on the column under spoken. This way all your examples will be from the spoken sub-registers in COCA. (See Figure 3.9.)

Take each one of the 100 samples you get this way and classify each bundle according to its position in the sentence. You can use the following categories: a) sentence initially; that is, when the bundle is the first four words in the sentence or utterance (for spoken); b) sentence finally; that is, when the bundle is the last four words in the sentence or utterance (for spoken); and c) neither sentence initially nor sentence finally; that is, when neither a) or b) applies. Use Table 3.5 to record the results. (See Figure 3.10 for concordance lines for "on the other hand".)

As a next step, do the same with academic prose to get your samples from that register. Then classify each of the 100 examples as one of the three categories above. Finally, calculate the percent value for each. (Note: Since you had 100 observations for each register, the percent value and the raw counts are the same.) Reset the sample size to 200, run it again, and see whether your results are similar.

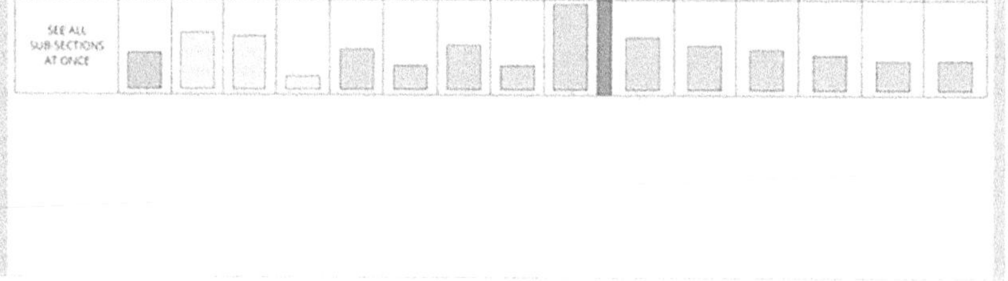

Figure 3.9 Distributional patterns of the 4-gram "on the other hand" in COCA

As a final note to this section, the longer the n-gram, or the word sequence, the less frequently it will occur simply because n-grams are embedded in one another. For example, in the four-word sequence *on the other hand*, the three-word sequences of *on the other* and *the other hand* are both present. These would be counted as two separate three-word sequences.

3.3.5 Five- and More-Grams

When you are extracting n-grams from a corpus, you can imagine that your sequences could be endless. However, that is not true. First, all three-word sequences will contain all the two-word sequences in them. Similarly, if you look at four-word sequences, they will have all the three-word sequences in them (and the two-word ones as well). Therefore, the higher the *n* is in your n-gram, the less frequency you will get for each sequence. This is particularly relevant in lexical bundles where it is not just the sequence that is part of the definition of a bundle but the cut-off point counts as well.

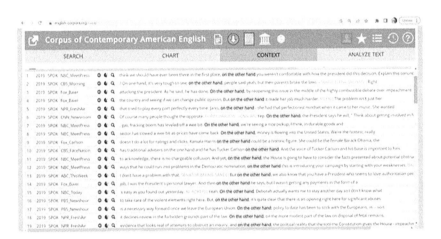

Figure 3.10 Concordance lines for the 4-gram "on the other hand" in COCA

Table 3.5 Distribution of the sentence position of "on the other hand" in spoken and written discourse

	Sentence-initial raw count (percent)	Sentence-final raw count (percent)	Other raw count (percent)	Total raw count (percent)
Spoken				100 (100)
Written				100 (100)

To illustrate this, we ran a lexical bundle search in a corpus of webtexts. This was a 1-million-word corpus of cybertexts collected from five internet registers: pop culture news, advertising, forum requests for advice, blogs, and tweets (Connor-Linton, 2012). Csomay and Cortes (2014) reported on the lexical bundles of four to eight words found in these five registers and examined their functions. They compared the webtext functions with those found in non-electronic registers (e.g., referential bundles, discourse organizers, and stance markers) and highlighted those that they found specific to these electronic registers (e.g., descriptive, narrative). The following four-word bundles were found unique to the webtexts: *what do you think*, *do you have any*, *I am trying to figure out*, *a recommended eBay seller*. And the following five-word bundles were found unique to the webtexts: *what do you think of*, *I just added myself to*, *made in the US and*, *originally posted by White Tiger*. The only one six-word bundle to meet the frequency requirement (at least ten times in a million words and in five different texts) to make it a bundle was: *I just updated my Squidoo page*. Finally, the two longest n-grams meeting the requirement to be a lexical bundle (at least ten times in a million words and in five texts) in this register were a seven-word bundle, *This article was originally published on Engineeringtalk*, mostly occurring in advertisements, and an eight-word bundle, *A free brochure or catalogue is available from*, also from an advertisement.

Project 3:18: Webtext Bundles

GlobWbe is an additional corpus on the website that contains texts from the internet. Check whether the webtext bundles reported above are present in all and with what frequency. In COCA, you can download the n-grams found up to 5-grams at their site with a specific n-grams website here: www.ngrams.info/samples_words.asp

3.4 POS Tags

Marking the words with part of speech (POS) tags [n, v, j, r] can lead us to different types of analyses than those we have seen so far. For example, you can look for specific words and their associated grammatical patterns or you can look for (co-occurring) grammatical patterns independent of the actual words. On the one hand, POS tags can help you be more specific about the words you are searching if you are going through an already existing search engine and if you are searching a corpus that has been tagged for part of speech. On the other hand, POS tags can also give you more options and more flexibility in your search. Below are examples of each. There are many other part of speech categories that could be potentially interesting for any linguistic study, but before going into some analyses we can do when we work with tags, let's clarify some basic grammar.

Each part of speech belongs to one of two basic classes: open or closed. Those part of speech categories that belong to the open class contain an unlimited number of members in them. That is, there is not a set number of members for an open class POS. There can be as many as there are in a language and we do not know how many there are. In contrast, those POSs that belong to the closed class have the characteristic to contain a limited number of members and we know exactly what they are. As another way to understand this distinction, note that we frequently have new open class words coming into the language, but the same is not the case with closed class words – new closed class words are quite rare.

Examples of POS belonging to the open category are the four main parts of speech: nouns, adjectives, verbs, and adverbs. Typically, nouns [n] are modified by adjectives [j], as in, for example, *big red car* where *big* is a characteristic of the noun in terms of its size, and *red* is a characteristic of the noun, telling us the color of the noun, and *car* is a common noun. Verbs [v] are modified by adverbs [r], as in, for example, *he drove fast* where *drove* is a verb – in past tense – and *fast* is an adverb modifying the verb by telling us how the action expressed by the verb is done. Examples of POS belonging to the closed category are many, and we only mention a few examples here to illustrate the point. These are: pronouns [pro], as in *he, she, it, their, him*, etc.; determiners [d], such as *this, that*, etc.; or conjunctions (both clausal and phrasal) such, as, *and, but, because*, etc., and many more.

Whether a POS belongs to the open or closed class, there are endless possibilities to search for association patterns, as shown in Chapter 2. As we have also seen in that chapter, the co-occurring patterns of these categories are the most interesting types of studies from the perspective of register variation because they are able to provide us with more comprehensive and detailed analyses of texts. Now, some corpora (e.g., COCA) have POS tags attached to each word, and some corpora (e.g., Michigan Corpus of Academic Spoken English [MICASE], and Michigan Corpus of Undergraduate Student Papers [MICUSP]) do not have that feature in addition to the actual words in a corpus. Some scholars find it more difficult to do a search on POS tags, and others write their own computer programs to process and count the different grammatical patterns through those tags.

3.4.1 Specifying POS for a Word

First, let's see how specifying part of speech categories with POS tags can help you be more specific about your search words. In the previous section, we compared the use of *state* and *say* in spoken and written registers. Go to COCA, hit "Browse" and type in *say* in the word box. Select all four part of speech categories. As you will see (also in Figure 3.11), the word *say* appears as a verb 4,096,146 times and ranks as the 26th most frequently occurring word in COCA. As a noun, it occurs 10,357 times and ranks as the 5,520th word for its frequency in COCA. When you go to the concordance lines, you will see that verbs are marked by the pink color (on the site). Now, type in *state*, and you will see that, similarly, the word *state* can be used as a verb or a noun but with different rankings and different frequencies. Clearly, when you compare the frequencies of these words in spoken and written discourse, you want to compare the instances in both cases only when they are used as verbs. Otherwise, you would be comparing apples with oranges. Because COCA contains POS tags, you can uncheck the boxes for all other possible POS categories (see the "Part of Speech" or POS button to the right of the search box) that you are not interested in when searching for the verb function in your comparison.

Using POS tags can broaden your options of looking for patterns – that is, how this will give you more options and more flexibility in your search. These main POS categories identify the word as you type it into the search box. Through the tags, however, we are able to look for variation within POS categories as well. The tags, for example, allow you to look for a given word in different word classes, such as *can* as a noun and *can* as a modal verb. Another example of what tags can do could be if you would like to look at a specific verb but you are only interested in the past tense forms, or if you want to search for exact examples of a particular noun but only in its plural form. To do this type of search, you can use POS codes, such as [v?d*] (e.g., *ate, drank, looked,* etc.) and [*nn2*] (e.g., *houses* or

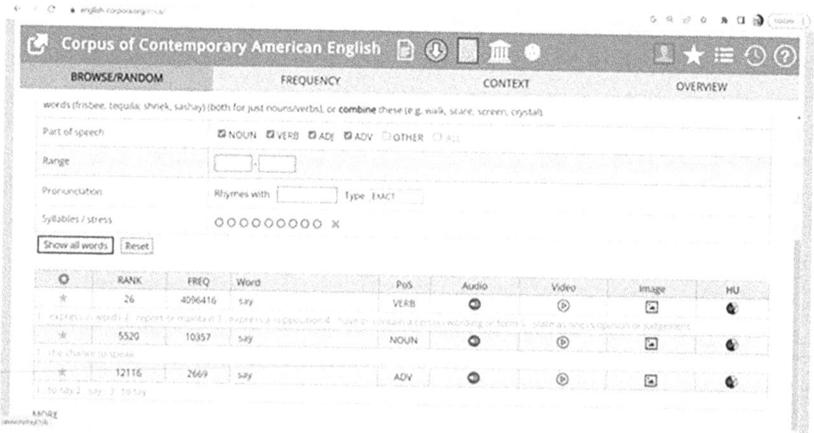

Figure 3.11 Frequency search in Word and Phrase

backyards), respectively. (Note: Don't forget to add the square brackets as that marks the fact that you are looking for POS categories and not words.)

Now go to COCA, and type in [v?d*] in the search window. This search will provide you with all the past tense verbs in the corpus ranked by frequency. Now if you tried [*nn2*], what do you think you will get? (See all POS tags used in COCA via the help menu.)

The third possibility is to see how often a specific word comes about in texts with different word forms. In the previous examples, we looked at *say* as a verb. In COCA, you would be typing the following string into the search box: say.[v*]. This indicates that you want to search and see the word *say* in this form and when it is a verb. What if you want to find out how often the verb *say* is used in past tense because you would like to make a comparison between the past tense use of *say* across four registers or see the syntactic position of the past tense use of *say*. Type the following into the search box: [say].[v*] (note the brackets around *say*). What kind of information do you get? This time, if the word is in square brackets, you work with the lemma of the word (i.e., the base form of the word), but you allow the inflections to be listed as well (such as past tense markers, third person "s" marker, etc.) What you see then is that the program divides the frequencies of the lexical verb *say* into the different verb forms, including past tense and third person singular, etc., and reports on the results accordingly. Click on the link "SAID" which will pull up all the examples of the word with this form, should you need textual examples.

The fourth option could be that you have an n-gram (e.g., a lexical bundle) and you want to see what kinds of words precede or follow that sequence. Let's try this with *if you look at*.

Project 3.19: "If You Look at" What?

Go through the following steps in completing this task:

Step 1: Go to COCA. Type in the search box *if you look at [nn*]*, click on "Chart,". You will see that in total, this bundle with a noun occurs 718 times in the entire corpus and 0.72 times in a million words. It is also apparent that about half of them occur in spoken discourse. Click on the SPOK bar to get the concordance lines. This will give you all the possible nouns following the bundle *if you look at* in spoken discourse.

Step 2: Go to a descriptive English reference grammar such as Biber et al. (1999) *Longman Grammar of English* or Biber et al. (2002) *Student Grammar of Spoken and Written English* and make a list of the categories for nouns (pp. 56–64 in the 2002 book). Now, look at the nouns that follow the lexical bundle you searched for, and classify the nouns in the categories you have set up. Can you see any patterns? That is, can you see any one semantic category that seems to occur more often than others? Report on your results.

Step 3: Take 30 randomly selected samples for the newspaper listing and 30 randomly selected samples from the spoken corpora listing. Compare the kinds of nouns following the bundle *if you look at*. Based on the examples you see, can you draw any conclusion whether, in your sample, there is evidence that one register may use more of certain types of nouns than the other with this bundle?

Step 4: Finally, just for fun, type in the search box *if you look at [n*]*, and click on "chart" and then go back and click on "KWIC" (after you click on the little + sign in the top row). How did your list change from the one you generated by doing Step 1 above?

Notes

1 These are normed counts to 1 million words – see about norming and why it is important in Chapter 6.
2 These numbers might change depending on updates in COCA. The current numbers were retrieved in June 2023.

References

Bednarek, M. (2010). *The language of fictional television: Drama and identity.* Continuum.

Bednarek, M. (2011). The stability of the televisual character: A corpus stylistic case study. In R. Piazza, M. Bednarek, & F. Rossi (Eds.), *Telecinematic discourse: Approaches to the language of films and television series* (pp. 185–204). John Benjamins.

Biber, D. (2009). A corpus-driven approach to formulaic language in English: Multi-word patterns in speech and writing. *International Journal of Corpus Linguistics, 14,* 275–311.

Biber, D., & Barbieri, F. (2007). Lexical bundles in university spoken and written registers. *English for Specific Purposes, 26,* 263–286.

Biber, D., & Conrad, S. (1999). Lexical bundles in conversation and academic prose. In H. Hasselgard & S. Oksefjell (Eds.), *Out of corpora* (pp. 81–190). Rodopi.

Biber, D., Conrad, S., & Leech, G. (2002). *Longman student grammar of spoken and written English.* Longman.

Biber, D., Conrad, S., & Cortes, V. (2004). "If you look at ...": Lexical Bundles in university teaching and textbooks. *Applied Linguistics, (25)*3, 371–405.

Biber, D., Johansson, S., Leech, G., Conrad, S., & Finegan, E. (1999) *Longman grammar of spoken and written English.* Longman.

Bondi, M. (2010). Perspectives on keywords and keyness. In M. Bondi & M. Scott (Eds.), *Keyness in texts* (pp. 1–20). John Benjamins.

Connor-Linton, J. (2012, March). "Multiple perspectives on analysis of webtexts", Colloquium presentation at Georgetown University Round Table, Georgetown.

Cortes, V. (2014, September). "Analyzing the structures, semantic prosodies, and semantic preferences of lexical bundles in research article introductions", Paper presented at the Conference for the American Association of Corpus Linguistics (AACL), Flagstaff, Arizona.

Cortes, V. (2015). Situating lexical bundles in the formulaic language spectrum. In V. Cortes & E. Csomay (Eds.), *Corpus-based research in Applied Linguistics. Studies in honor of Doug Biber* (pp. 197–216). John Benjamins.

Csomay, E. (2013). Lexical bundles in discourse structure: A corpus-based study of classroom discourse. *Applied Linguistics 34*(3), 369–388.

Csomay, E., & Young, R. (2021). Language use in pop culture over three decades: A diachronic keyword analysis of *Star Trek* dialogues. In M. Bednarek, V. Werner, & M. Pinto (Eds.), *Telecinematic discourse.* Special issue of *International Journal of Corpus Linguistics*, 26(1), 71–94.

Csomay, E., & Cortes, V. (2014, September). "Lexical bundles in cybertexts" Paper presented at the Conference for the American Association of Corpus Linguistics (AACL), Flagstaff, Arizona.

Culpeper, J. (2009). Keyness: Words, parts-of-speech and semantic categories in the character talk of Shakespeare's *Romeo and Juliet. International Journal of Corpus Linguistics*, 14(1), 29–59.

Culpeper, J., & Demmen, J. (2015). Keywords. In D. Biber & R. Reppen (Eds.), *The Cambridge handbook of Corpus Linguistics* (pp. 90–105). Cambridge University Press.

Firth, J.R. (1951). *Modes of meaning. Essays and studies of the English Association* [NS 4], 118–149.

Fischer-Starcke, B. (2009). Keywords and frequent phrases of Jane Austen's *Pride and Prejudice*: A corpus-stylistic analysis. *International Journal of Corpus Linguistics*, 14(4), 492–523.

Phillips, M. (1985). *Aspects of text structure: An investigation of the lexical organization of text.* North Holland.

Scott, M. (1997). PC analysis of key words – and key key words. *System, 25*(2), 233–245.

Scott, M., & Tribble, C. (2006). *Textual Patterns: Key words and corpus analysis in language education.* John Benjamins.

Williams, R. (1986). *Keywords.* Fontana.

Chapter 4

Projects Using Publicly Available Corpora

4.1 Word- and Phrase-Based Projects
4.2 Grammar-Based Projects

This chapter provides you with an opportunity to use readily available corpora to conduct corpus linguistics projects. In this chapter, you will gain practical experience in using corpus linguistic methodologies and interpreting results. There is a total of ten projects in this chapter with some comments for each project that can guide your analysis. Because there are different ways to conduct analyses with respect to search procedures and analyses, the projects do not have a single correct answer. At the end of each project, we provide commentary for those who may seek more guidance on how to search and interpret findings.

The projects in this chapter use four different corpora that are found on English-Corpora.org (www.english-corpora.org/), an online resource for corpora that is updated regularly and is an excellent resource for getting started working with corpora. Our decision to use this resource is related to cost, accessibility, and coverage. Although you need to register in order to use the corpus, as we mentioned in the previous chapter, access to the corpora is free of charge. Every 10–15 searches you will receive a message asking you to subscribe but subscription is optional. If you choose to subscribe, the current price (2023) is 30.00 USD which is quite cost-effective for the available corpora and data. Institutional licenses are also available so check with your school whether they have an institutional subscription. In addition to being reasonably priced, these corpora have a number of advantages for researchers, teachers, and students of language studies. The corpora include different varieties of English, including American (Corpus of Contemporary American English), British (British National Corpus), and Canadian (Strathy Corpus). There are also corpora focusing specifically on news found on the web (iWeb, GloWbE, Core) as well as television shows, movies, and soap operas. All of the corpora are in English but many of them include different varieties of English. For example, GloWbE contains

DOI: 10.4324/9781003363309-6

web news from 20 different countries which permits investigations related to variation across different varieties of English. All of the corpora also use the same search interface so that once you learn how to "ask" for information in one corpus, you can conduct searches in all of the available corpora. The home page also includes many helpful resources and videos to guide you in the use of the corpus and use of search terms. There is even a link to training videos for people who are unable to access YouTube.

A list of the corpora we will use for the corpus projects in this chapter is provided in Table 4.1 but the entire list of corpora can be found at: www. english-corpora.org/.

There are a few important points to remember about these corpora that are especially true when conducting projects that compare features across different corpora or when looking at register differences. First, the corpus sizes range from the 1.9-billion-word GloWbE corpus to the 50-million-word Strathy corpus. This means that if one is comparing a different feature across different corpora, frequency comparisons refer to normalized counts. Another important aspect to keep in mind relates to different registers in the corpora. Some corpora (GloWbE and COHA) are comprised of a single register; other corpora (COCA and BNC) contain multiple registers. Even within a single register, there are situational differences that need to be carefully considered. For example, in the BNC, the spoken data include contexts such as oral histories, meetings, lectures, and doctor–patient interactions. In COCA, the spoken examples are all taken from television and radio news and information shows. These different situational variables mean that the term "spoken language" may mean (i.e., represent) different things in different corpora. It is important to understand the situational characteristics of the texts when representing a register (as we discussed in Chapter 2). These potential differences need to be considered when comparing and interpreting language features across corpora. Even though both COCA and the BNC contain a "spoken" component, there are many situational differences between news shows and face-to-face conversation (for one, news shows display grammatical features that are characteristic of more informational

Table 4.1 Information on corpora used for projects in this chapter

Name of Corpus	# of words	Language/dialect variety	Time period
Global Web-Based English (GloWbE)	1.9 billion	20 countries	2012–13
Corpus of Contemporary American English (COCA)	1 billion	American	1990–2019
Corpus of Historical American English (COHA)	475 million	American	1810–2019
British National Corpus (BNC)	100 million	British	1980s–1993

types of discourse while face-to-face conversation displays features that have been associated with more involved or interactional types of discourse; cf. Biber, 1995) that would account for differences in language features. Consequently, any differences in the spoken register of these corpora need to be understood in relation to the spoken contexts used in the corpus. A feature may be related to spoken language in news and information broadcasts but not found in other spoken contexts such as face-to-face conversation so, in many respects, the spoken corpora of COCA and the BNC may not be comparable (i.e., they do not represent the same thing).

4.1 Word- and Phrase-Based Projects

Project 4.1: Lexical Change Over Time

The Corpus of Contemporary American English (COCA) corpus is divided into different time periods. Find five words that are recent (have a higher frequency in the most recent time period) and five examples of words that are more common in the earliest time period. For the more recent words, is there a steady growth curve or does the word gain popularity fairly rapidly (i.e., in a single time period)? For the declining words, is there a steady decline or a fairly rapid decline? What are some possible reasons for these tendencies you have found?

Comment: For this exercise, you may want to think of words related to technology, political events, or social trends. For example, if you were to look at "text" as a verb, you would see that this verb has increased from 1990 to 2020 while "fax" has moved in the opposite direction. In addition to the frequency of the word over time, you may also consider how the word is used. Do the connotations of the word remain the same over time? Are there any new meanings associated with these words?

Project 4.2: Meanings of "Literally"

The word *literally* was originally used to mean something similar to *exactly*, *precisely*, or *actually*. In this sense of the word, the meaning is closely related to the concept of something being free from metaphor. This meaning is understood in a sentence such as:

> *I've literally spent more holidays with the animals than I have with my own family.*

(example taken from COCA)

In addition to this meaning of the word *literally*, there is another sense of the word that shows emphasis (with a meaning similar to *really*). This sense of the word is sometimes the opposite of "being free from metaphor" as in a sentence such as:

There's a story about this in this book and it blows my mind, literally.
(example taken from COCA)

Using COCA, determine the variation in use of both the literal and figurative sense of the word *literally* by completing the following steps:

Step 1: Develop and state your method for determining whether the word falls into the "literal" category or the "non-literal" category. Do you find any other senses of the word that do not fit into your two categories? If so, describe the extra category or categories you have found and provide examples to support each category. Then, determine whether one sense of the word is more frequent.

Step 2: Register differences: Using the chart function, describe the distribution of *literally* across the different registers. Are there some registers where this word is used more than other registers? What are some potential reasons for any differences? Using the method you have developed in Step 1, do you find any register differences in the meanings of *literally* across registers?

Step 3: Looking at the distribution of *literally* across time periods in COCA, do you find any historical trends in the frequency of the word? Is there an increase in the different senses of the word *literally* over time?

Comment: Using the word search function will provide many examples (over 39,000) that may be difficult to interpret without some systematic way of analyzing the word. To narrow your search and make an analysis more manageable, you can choose a smaller number of texts to analyze or even create a smaller, virtual corpus. These are both explained in the "KWIC → analyze texts" option under the "guides" tab on the home page. For Steps 1 and 2, you can get a general overview of the word by choosing "search" and then "word". This provides information such as register frequency, meanings, topics, collocates by word class, frequent clusters containing *literally*, concordance lines, and references to entire texts that contain the word. For Step 3, make sure that you are still using the COCA corpus and have selected "chart" in the search.

Project 4.3: "Gate" as Post-Fix for Any Accepted Problem After the Term "Watergate"

In addition to its contribution to the demise of the presidency of Richard Nixon, the so-called Watergate Scandal has contributed to the American lexicon through the use of the suffix *-gate* added to describe controversial political or social incidents. In this project, you will explore the different ways this suffix has been used in American English and look at other language varieties to see if this suffix is also found in other varieties of English. Complete the following steps:

Step 1: Using COCA, identify at least six cases where this suffix is used with a noun. For each, note its first appearance; then note when each term was most frequently used and whether it is still used today.

Step 2: Use GloWbE to determine whether this suffix is also found in other varieties of English.

Step 3: Interpret your results: What are some possible reasons for your findings? Are there other examples of prefixes or suffixes that are specific to varieties of English?

Comment: A search using the wildcard * + *gate* will yield a list of words containing *-gate*. These include the word *gate* as well as words such as *investigate* and *promulgate*. You will also find words such as *travelgate* and *pizzagate* that are more relevant. From this list, you can then select specific instances of the word that use this suffix. When using other corpora, you may either search for the exact words you found in COCA or use the same wildcard search to see if there are specific uses of *-gate* in the other corpora you have used. Using the latter approach will identify any creative uses of the suffix.

Project 4.4: Clichés

Owen Hargraves has written a book titled *It's Been Said Before: A Guide to the Use and Abuse of Clichés* (2014). In the introduction of this book, Hargraves states:

> While it is true that a vast number of expressions have become tired through overuse, there is an opportunity to make even the most worn expressions striking and powerful. How do we decide which among many expressions might be just right for the occasion, or just wrong?
>
> (p. xi)

In this project, we will take a close look at some of the clichés Hargraves mentions in his book. Complete the following steps:

Step 1: Come up with a "working definition" of a cliché. How has the concept of a cliché been defined? Is there general agreement on what a cliché is? What differences in definitions do you note?

Step 2: Use the "search" and "word" functions to inform your working definition. Specifically, how does the topic, collocate (what nouns, verbs, adjectives, and adverbs occur most frequently with *cliché*?) and cluster information help in defining your definition?

Step 3: Using both COCA and the BNC, provide the normalized frequency of each of the phrases below:

dizzying array	meteoric rise	point the finger
perfect storm	touch and go	totally awesome

What do these frequencies tell you about the relationship between these clichés and American and British English?

1. Are there specific registers that use these phrases more frequently than other registers? What might be some reasons for any differences you find?
2. Given your working definition of a cliché, would you define any or all of the six examples as clichés? Are there other examples that are more representative of clichés?

Comment: In addition to deciding if these six phrases are all clichés, you may also want to consider the extent to which these phrases are fixed. For example, you can search for the most frequent collocate that occurs after *dizzying* or the most frequent collocate that occurs before *array* (make sure to choose the first slot to the right or left of these words). Doing this for many of these phrases can provide information on how frequently these words collocate. This approach is easier to do with phrases that do not have function words (*touch and go*; *point the finger*) since there will be many more words that precede and follow function words such as the function words *and/the*.

Project 4.5: Collocation of Modifying Elements

In this project, you will look at the most common words that follow the modifiers below.

categorically   *deeply*   *entirely*   *far-reaching*   *massively*

You will use COCA, the BNC, and GloWbE. Complete the following steps in the project.

Step 1: For both COCA and the BNC, determine the most common word that follows each of the terms above. You can do this by using the

"COLLOCATES" function; set the span to "0" on the left and "1" on the right.

Step 2: What similarities and differences in the two language varieties do you find in the types of words that follow the modifiers?

Step 3: Use GloWbE to determine the most common collocate of the five modifiers above. Using the patterns you found for both American and British English, try to find a language variety that patterns like American English and a language variety that patterns like British English for each of the five modifiers. What factors might influence these language varieties to pattern like American or British English? Do you find any patterns that are unlike both American and British English? What are some possible reasons for any new patterns that you find?

Comment: When searching for these modifiers, note the frequency of each word. What are the most common and least common modifiers? Do the frequency counts for these words stay the same across language varieties? Additionally, when looking at collocates of these words, pay attention to the types of words that are found to the right. Are all the words adjectives or are there other word types (e.g., verbs) found as a right collocate?

Project 4.6: Sustainability

According to the *Oxford English Dictionary* (www.oed.com), the adjective *sustainable* originally referred to the ability to endure something. In this definition it was synonymous with the adjective *bearable*. Although this use of the term is now quite rare, there are other meanings of *sustainable* that are more commonly used in English. These definitions are provided below (definitions are quoted from www.oed.com):

1. Capable of being upheld or defended as valid, correct, or true
2a. Capable of being maintained or continued at a certain rate or level
2b. Designating forms of human activity (esp. of an economic nature) in which environmental degradation is minimized, esp. by avoiding the long-term depletion of natural resources; of or relating to activity of this type. Also: designating a natural resource which is exploited in such a way as to avoid its long-term depletion.

In this project, you will use both COHA (Corpus of Historical American English) and COCA to investigate these different meanings of the word *sustainable* (and its noun counterpart, *sustainability*) over time and across registers. Complete the following steps:

Step 1: Using COHA, note the first 50 occurrences of the adjective *sustainable*. For each use, provide the date of occurrence and note which of the three definitions provided above best fit with the occurrence of the word. Make sure to provide examples from the corpus to support your analysis of their meanings. Is one use of *sustainable* more prevalent than other uses of it? Is there a tendency for the meaning to change over time?

Step 2: Using COCA, note the register distribution of the adjective *sustainable*. In which registers is *sustainable* most common? In which registers is *sustainable* less common? Are there specific meanings of *sustainable* that are representative of specific registers? Provide some reasons for any register or meaning differences that you find. Make sure to support your analysis with examples from the corpus.

Step 3: This part of the project asks you to look at the meanings and register distribution of the noun *sustainability*. According to the online site "Environmental Leader":

> Sustainability includes sustainable building, design and operations. Sustainability is the collection of policies and strategies employed by companies to minimize their environmental impact on future generations. Ecological concerns, such as the environmental impact of pollutants, are balanced with socio-economic concerns such as minimizing the consumption of limited natural resources to maintain their availability for the future.
>
> (www.environmentalleader.com/category/sustainability/)

Using COHA, note the first 20 occurrences of the word *sustainability*. For each use, provide the date of occurrence and note which of the three definitions provided above best fit with the occurrence of the word. Make sure to provide examples from the corpus to support your analysis of their meanings. In which registers is *sustainability* most common? In which registers is *sustainability* less common? Provide some reasons for any register distribution differences that you find. Do the meanings of sustainability all relate to environmental or ecological issues or are there other senses of the word that are found in COCA?

Comment: It is possible to search for the most common nouns following *sustainable* using <sustainable NOUN+>. For *sustainability*, using the first left collocate function will provide a list of the most common adjectives preceding *sustainability*. It may also be helpful to use the "compare" function to investigate any synonyms of *sustainable/sustainability*. Do *sustainable/sustainability* have any viable synonyms?

Project 4.7: "Frugal", "Cheap", and "Thrifty"

In this project, we will consider different connotations of the adjectives *cheap*, *frugal*, and *thrifty*. We will also look at how these words may differ in their syntactic positions. There are a group of adjectives in English that can occur in both pre-noun and post-verbal positions. For example, the adjective *little* can be used in the sentence *The little house is painted blue* as well as in the sentence *The house is little*. In the first sentence, the adjective *little* is called an "attributive" adjective (i.e., it occurs in the attributive [pre-noun] position); in the second sentence, the adjective is called a "predicative" adjective (i.e., it occurs in the predicative [post-verbal] position). Not all adjectives have such a freedom of movement to these different positions. For example, the adjective *upset* generally is found in the predicative position (*The man is upset*) and may sound odd in the attributive position (*The upset man left the library*).

This project will consider the connotations of a group of adjectives that can occur in both attributive and predicative positions. We will start this project by considering the following letter that appeared in "Dear Abby" on March 20, 2015:

DEAR ABBY: *My wife, "Tina", was very hurt by a friend recently. Her friend "Sally" called her "cheap" during a conversation ("she's cheap like you"). Sally didn't intend it to be hurtful, just an illustration – but my wife is very upset about it. We use coupons when we grocery shop or dine out; we also watch our thermostats, recycle, etc. On the other hand, we have sent our children to university without loans, our mortgage is paid off, we have traveled extensively and our net worth is north of a million dollars with no debt. How do I make Tina realize that Sally's comment should not upset her so? – THRIFTY IN TEXAS.*

DEAR THRIFTY: *What happened was unfortunate because the problem may be that Sally simply chose the wrong word. What she probably meant was that your wife is frugal. The difference between "frugal" and "cheap" is that being frugal is a virtue. Because Sally hurt your wife's feelings, Tina needs to tell her how it made her feel so Sally can apologize to her before it causes a permanent rift.*

This letter (as well as Abby's response to it) illustrates the social impact that synonymous words may have on some people. "Thrifty in Texas" seeks advice to help his wife understand that their friend, Sally, did not intend to offend her. Abby's response indicates that Sally merely chose the incorrect word and perhaps should have selected a synonym of "cheap" that indicated the positive aspects of saving money. This project will consider 1) what a corpus might tell us about the meanings of the adjectives *cheap*, *frugal*, and *thrifty*; and 2) whether these three synonyms share similar syntactic characteristics. Complete all steps in the analysis.

Step 1: Using COCA, report on the frequency and distribution of the adjectives *cheap*, *frugal*, and *thrifty*. Which of these words is the most frequent, and which of these words are less frequent? Are there any register differences in the distribution of these words? If so, what are some possible reasons for any register differences?

Step 2: Using the "KWIC" and "COLLOCATES" functions, explain any differences in meaning among these three words. Do some words have a more positive or negative connotation than other words? If so, what evidence can you provide to support your answer? Make sure to use examples to back up your analysis.

Step 3: Using the "POS" function in COCA, determine whether each of these three adjectives is more common in attributive or predicative position. Do all three adjectives have similar syntactic distributions? Are there differences in meaning when the same word is in a different syntactic position? Make sure that you use examples to support your analysis. Also, make sure that you include all of the search terms that you have used.

Step 4: Given what you now know about the different meanings and syntactic positions of the adjectives *cheap*, *frugal*, and *thrifty*, write a response to "Thrifty in Texas" that might provide some helpful advice for how to address his problem.

Comments: In Step 2, you can use the "compare" function and look at the most common words to the left and right of the adjectives. This option allows you to control the number of words to the left and right. Choosing the words directly before or after the adjective will tell you about any potential collocations; choosing a larger span will tell you more about the other types of words that are semantically associated with each adjective. In Step 3, one possible search string for the attributive position is looking for all verbs before the adjective (e.g., <VERB thrifty>) or all nouns following the adjective (e.g., <NOUN cheap>).

4.2 Grammar-Based Projects

Project 4.8: Variation in the Passive Voice

There are two main "voices" in English. In grammar terms, voice refers to the relationship between the verb of a sentence and the other participants, such as the subject and the object of a sentence. In a sentence such as *The boy saw the ghost* (an active voice sentence), we know who sees the ghost (the subject of the sentence, *the boy*) and who is seen (the object of the sentence, *the ghost*). In this sense, the subject noun phrase *the boy* serves as the "actor" of the sentence (the one doing the action of the verb) and the noun phrase object *the ghost* serves as the "patient" or "recipient" of the action (the receiver of the action). The second type of voice in English is called the passive voice. For example, in a sentence such as *The boy is seen by the ghost*, even though *the boy* is still in the subject position of the sentence, it is *the ghost* who is doing the seeing in this type of sentence. Consequently, the voice of the sentence provides information on who or what is doing the action and who or what is affected by the action expressed by the verb. The passive voice is formed by adding an auxiliary verb (*be*) to the passive voice sentence and substituting the "regular" form of the verb with the past participle. You will be asked to look at this rule a bit closer in the project below.

Another noteworthy aspect of the passive voice includes variation in the extent to which the original actor of the sentence (the subject of the active voice sentence) is present in the passive voice sentence. For example, compare the active voice *The girl broke the window* with its passive voice counterpart, *The window was broken (by the girl)*. In this passive voice sentence, there are two options, one that states who broke the window and another that doesn't state the subject by the deletion of the entire "by phrase" (e.g., *The window was broken*). We can call the first of these passive types, the long passive (a passive sentence that includes the "by phrase"), and the second type, the short passive (a passive sentence without the "by phrase").

In addition to the verb *be*, the passive voice can also be expressed by the auxiliary verb *get*. See Table 4.2 for examples of the two auxiliaries.

Using COCA, compare the two forms of the passive, initially concentrating on the two auxiliary verbs *was* and *got* by using the search strings *was _v?n* and *got _v?n)*.

1. Which of these two types of passive is more common overall? Are there register differences between the two passive types? What possible reasons might there be for any differences you have found?
2. Is there a difference in the verbs used in *was* passives versus *got* passives? How would you describe these differences?

Table 4.2 Passive voice

Subject	Auxiliary verb	Main verb	By phrase
John	was	stopped	by the police
John	got	stopped	by the police

3. Choose five different *was* passives and five different *got* passives. For
    each type, determine whether there is a preference for the "by phrase".
    Does your data suggest that the "by phrase" is dependent on the verb,
    on the auxiliary verb, or is it due to some other factor?

Comment: In addition to passive voice differences between *was* and got,
it is also possible to include different forms of the auxiliary verb in your
analysis. This can be done by replacing *was* with *is/are/ being* or *got* with
gets/getting. Alternatively, the lemma of each verb can be used by using the
search terms BE _v?n or GET -v?n. Using this approach will provide some
non-passive examples such as *get rid of* which should not be included in
the analysis.

Project 4.9: "Going to" as a Modal Verb

In the two sentences below, the underlined words *going to* are different
types of grammatical constructions. In the first, *going* is the main verb of
the clause and *to* is a preposition that is followed by a noun phrase (*the
loo*); in the second sentence, *going to* precedes the verb *go*. One way to
show this difference is to determine when *going to* can be contracted or
simplified to *gonna*. It is possible to use *gonna* in the second sentence but
not the first sentence.

(a) *My father is up all night going to the loo which keeps both him and my
     mother awake.*
(b) *Yet not everyone is going to go to college, develop software skills, or
     become an entrepreneur.*

(examples from COCA)

The difference between these two examples illustrates the descriptive observation that in cases where a contraction is permissible, the *going to* is function-
ing as a modal verb; in cases where *gonna* is not possible, the construction is
comprised of a main verb (*going*) followed by a prepositional phrase. In this
project, you will examine the modal verb *going to* in detail. Complete the
following steps in your analysis of the modal verb *going to* (*gonna*).

Step 1: Determine the search term(s) you will use to find examples of *going
   to* followed by a verb (e.g., going to VERB)
Step 2: Use COHA and determine when this use came into the language.
   What patterns of development do you find? Are there certain verbs
   that tend to occur with *going to*? Have these verbs changed over time?
Step 3: Are there differences in the way the two forms of *going to* and
   gonna are used in COHA? What are some possible reasons for any
   differences you may find?

Step 4: Using COCA, do you see any register differences in the use of *going to* and *gonna* as a modal verb? If so, what are the differences you see? Try to provide some explanation for any register differences you may find.

Comment: Trying different search terms can be helpful in this project. Some possible search terms are: <BE going to> which provides all different forms of the verb *be* before *going to* (e.g., *are/is/were going to*). It is also possible to search for both <VERB going to> to find all verbs preceding *going to* and <going to NOUN> to find all nouns following *going to*. Similar searches can also be done with *gon na* (<VERB gon na> and <gon na NOUN> which can provide some very interesting results. Doing similar searches in GloWbE will also illustrate potential differences across different language varieties.

Project 4.10: Grammatical Constructions Following "Begin", "Continue", and "Start"

In English, there is a good deal of variation in the forms of non-finite grammatical clauses that follow (i.e., complement) verbs. The non-finite clauses in this project are the gerund (-ing) clause (a) and the infinitive (to) clause (b):

(a) *Chekesha was third at district last year and barely missed **going** to regionals.*
(b) *The study subjects were asked **to estimate** the surface normal at many points on the drawings.*

(examples from COCA)

Note that the infinitive clause is not a possible complement of *miss* (*... *missed to go to regionals*) and the gerund clause is not a possible complement of *ask* (*... *asked estimating the surface normal at many points on the drawings*). There are other verbs that allow both gerund and infinitive clauses as complements. The verb *start*, for example, allows both, as seen in (c) and (d).

(c) *When you start **looking** for things in love, there's nothing left to **find**.*
(d) *Hair can start **to lose** its luster and look dull and ashy ...*

(examples from COCA)

In this project, you will look at three verbs (*begin, continue,* and *start*) that allow both gerund and infinitive clauses in COCA. Complete all steps in the analysis.

Step 1: Using COCA, report on the complementation patterns of the three verbs (*begin, continue,* and *start*). How do the three verbs compare in their complementation patterns?

Step 2: For each of the three verbs, determine whether there are register differences in the patterns.

Step 3: What reasons account for the variation of complementation patterns in these three verbs?

Comment: Using the search pattern <continue to VERB> and <continue _ v?g> where you can substitute continue for both *start* and *begin* will provide relevant examples. The different patterns can be reported as percentages of infinitive (to VERB) and gerunds (-ing verbs) for *begin, continue,* and *start*. It may also be helpful to look for different types of verbs that are used in the different constructions. For example, what is the most common verb following *start to* versus *starting to* (and *begin to* versus *beginning to*; *continue to* versus *continuing to*)? Are there similarities and differences in the infinitive and gerund categories with respect to the specific verbs *begin, continue,* and *start* or are the differences more related to the infinitive and gerund categories and not the specific verbs themselves? Additionally, you may also include a discussion of *begin* and *start*. One might expect that because *begin* and *start* are virtually synonymous, they might pattern the same. Is this true? If they do not pattern the same, what are some possible reasons for the difference?

References

Biber, D. (1995). *Dimensions of register variation: A cross-linguistic perspective.* Cambridge University Press.

Hargraves, O. (2014). *It's been said before: A guide to the use and abuse of clichés.* Oxford University Press.

Part III

Building Your Own Corpus, Analyzing Your Quantitative Results, and Making Sense of Data

Chapter 5

Building Your Own Corpus

This chapter will take you through the steps to complete a corpus project. By reference to a specific research question, you will learn how to build your own corpus and then analyze it using both the register functional analysis approach covered in Chapter 2 and the corpus software programs covered in Chapter 3. You will also learn how to use AntConc in this chapter.

5.1 Do-It-Yourself Corpora

In the previous chapter, you were exposed to readily available corpora through the projects using the suite of corpora at English-corpora.org. These corpora can be used to explore language variation by reference to different situations of use, such as newspaper writing, fiction, and spoken language from news talk shows. These corpora are not, however, designed to understand language variation in other contexts that may also be of interest. For example, there is no easy way to determine information about the gender or age of those who produced the texts. If you were interested in looking at gender or age differences in language use, these corpora would not be of much use. Certain research questions require "specialized" corpora that are built for specific purposes. Sometimes researchers need to build their own corpora. Corpus building not only allows you to answer a specific research question, but it also gives you experience in corpus construction. There is likely no better way to learn about the issues in corpus design and to appreciate the larger corpora built by other researchers than

DOI: 10.4324/9781003363309-8

to build one on your own. Constructing a useful corpus involves a number of steps that are described below.

Before covering the steps in corpus building, we should acknowledge potential copyright issues. In some cases, you may use the internet for the texts to include in your corpus. In order to do this, you will need to carefully consider your selection of materials and the potential copyright infringement issues that relate to compiling and storing digital texts. Additionally, it is important to take into account the country in which the corpus materials are used. Different countries have different copyright rules. What might be considered a copyright infringement in one country may not be considered so in another country. If you are using the corpus for educational purposes and do not plan on selling the corpus or any information that would result from an analysis of the corpus (e.g., in publications), the likelihood of being prosecuted as a copyright violator is usually small. Nevertheless, you should take into account the following guidelines when building your own corpora:

- Make sure that your corpus is used for private study and research for a class or in some other educational context.
- Research presentations or papers that result from the research should not contain large amounts of text from the corpus. Concordance lines and short language samples (e.g., fewer than 25 words) are preferable over larger stretches of text.
- When compiling a corpus using resources from the internet, only use texts that are available to the public at no additional cost.
- Make sure that your corpus is not used for any commercial purposes.
- Make sure to acknowledge the sources of the texts that are in the corpus.

For those interested in more information on corpus building and copyright laws, there are some sources to consult at the end of this chapter.

5.2 Deciding on a Corpus Project

Corpus research projects take a good deal of time commitment to complete. A worthy research project has a number of different components, including providing a motivation of the significance of the topic, a clear description of the corpus and the methods used in the study, presentation of results, a discussion of the results, and a conclusion that provides a summary and "takeaway message" of the research. In Chapter 8, you will learn more about how to present your research as both a written report as well as an oral presentation. However, before embarking on this project, it is valuable to spend some time thinking seriously about what you want to research and the reasons for conducting the research; i.e., the research goal of the study. Selecting an appropriate research issue is not a trivial matter. A well-motivated research project not only contributes to the knowledge of the field but it will also hold your interest for the duration of the project (and perhaps even beyond the duration of the project). The corpus you will build depends on your research goal. If you are not clear about what you want to investigate (and why the research is worthy/ useful), it will be difficult to build a relevant corpus for the purpose of your research!

When deciding on a topic, you should choose a subject that is not only interesting to you but also potentially relevant to others. In other words, if you were to tell someone about your research topic and they were to say "So what?" you should have a well-reasoned response. To answer this question, try to choose a topic that you believe will contribute to the understanding of how and why language forms may vary in certain contexts. Some possible general topics could be:

- How does language vary in different groups of language users (e.g., British, American, Canadian, Sri Lankan, Indian, Chinese, Japanese users)?

    Do some types of English (such as Sri Lankan English or Japanese English) show similarities with other groups of English users (such as British or American English)?

- How does language use vary for people who have different political or religious beliefs?

    Do politically conservative and politically liberal groups use similar forms of language?

- How do song lyrics vary in different types of music?

    Do lyrics in hip hop songs use similar different forms of language than from lyrics in hard rock songs?

- How does the language of social media differ from written and/or spoken language?

    Are posts on social media sites such as Facebook or Twitter similar to spoken or written language?

- How does language used in "authentic" contexts compare to prescriptive views of language?

    Does newspaper language or academic writing follow the prescriptive rules found in usage manuals?

- Is there a relationship between gender identity and language use?

Are there differences in traditional binary gender distinctions and more nuanced perspectives of gender?

This list is not intended to be exhaustive. Each of the topics and subtopics described above address issues that are not specific to the field of corpus linguistics but lend themselves to corpus research quite well. For example, a topic examining gender differences could involve creating a corpus of fitness articles with females as the intended audience and comparing this to a corpus of fitness articles with males as the intended audience. A project looking at the language of social media posts could be achieved by creating a corpus of Twitter posts and comparing the language used in the posts with written or spoken language found in existing corpora such as the CORE corpus found English-corpus.org.

In addition to identifying a research goal, you should also write a research question or set of research questions that you seek to answer in your research. Because this book uses register analysis as a framework for interpreting your research, the research questions in your projects all share the similarity of investigating the extent to which situational variables result in different linguistic features for some functional reason. In this sense, all research questions are framed from a particular perspective by reference to a specific methodology (corpus linguistics). The research question of an individual study depends on the specific variables under investigation. Note that all of the research issues described above are in the form of questions. Each research topic has a corresponding question (or set of questions) or a hypothesis that will be answered in the research study.

Whatever issue you select, you should have a convincing explanation of your reason for conducting the research. The first questions you can ask about your project are: "What is my research goal?" and "Why was it important to conduct the research?" If you find, for example, that song lyrics have different linguistic characteristics in different types of music, what is the relevance of this finding? Does it say something about the possible socio-cultural aspects of the consumers of the music or does it say something about the music genre in general? Clear and convincing reasons for choosing a research topic will not only help you in motivating your research, but it will also help you in interpreting the results of your research. Worthy research topics do not need particular outcomes to be interesting or relevant. To use the example of song lyrics and musical varieties again, it would be just as interesting to find little difference in the linguistic characteristics of musical varieties as it would be to find strong differences.

A final consideration relates to the type of corpus that you will build to conduct your project. A vital part of your corpus project is, obviously, the corpus itself! Before deciding on a final topic, you should determine the availability of texts that will enable you to address the issue you propose to research. You will need to make sure that the types of texts you need to carry out your project are available free of charge (so as to decrease the chance of a copyright infringement).

Giving careful thought and consideration to the importance and relevance of your research topic (including a strong justification for your selection of a research topic, i.e., the motivation for your study) is more likely to result in a project that you are proud of and that contributes to an understanding of language variation. Taking the time to consider the significance of your project and its potential application to the field of applied linguistics (or other fields of study such as sociology, business, or art and music) is time well spent.

5.3 Building a Corpus

Once you have selected an adequate research goal and corresponding research question (or set of questions), the next step is to build a relevant corpus. The corpus that you will be building for your project will likely not be a large general corpus but will be a smaller, "specialized" corpus that is designed to answer the specific research question(s) you are investigating. One difference between specialized corpora and larger, more general corpora relates to their purpose: Specialized corpora are normally designed to address specific research questions while general corpora are intended for a larger audience and are designed to answer a larger set of research questions posed by multiple researchers. This is not to say that specialized corpora are never used to answer different research questions, but they generally are designed to investigate a restricted set of questions, and therefore, are less likely a representative of language use in general terms. As you will see further in the next chapters, with smaller, specialized corpora, you are only able to draw conclusions in your dataset rather than generalize the results to larger contexts. Even though smaller, specialized corpora are used for more restricted research purposes than general corpora, adopting a sound set of guidelines to build the corpus is still important. A well-designed corpus includes texts that are relevant to the research goals of the study; are saved into a file format that allows different software programs to analyze the texts; and are labeled with enough relevant contextual material so that the different contexts are easily identifiable in the corpus. We will take a closer look at each of these below.

The selection of the texts to include in your corpus depends on their suitability and their availability. Clearly, the texts need to share relevant characteristics (or variables) that meet your selection criteria for inclusion in the corpus. A project that considers how news writing changes in different time periods would, obviously, require a corpus that includes newspaper articles written at different periods of time. In order to build a corpus to address this issue, you would need to make sure that there is an adequate number of newspaper articles that have been written at different time periods. Additionally, a corpus addressing this issue would need to have sub-corpora of relatively equal size. As illustrated in some of the corpus projects that compared COCA with the BYU-BNC corpus, the unequal sizes of these two corpora did not allow for straight frequency comparisons between the two corpora. Thus, corpus "balance" is a key aspect of reliable corpus building. Note that the balance should consider not only the number of texts in each sub-corpus but should also consider the word count of the sub-corpora.

Frequency comparisons are done on the basis of the number of words, not by the number of texts. If your specialized corpus also contains sub-corpora, then you should ensure the sub-corpora is of fairly equal sizes. Another issue related to corpus balance in your corpus relates to text types. A news writing corpus would need to include the various types of news texts – sports and lifestyle news as well as state, local, national, and international news. If only one of these text types is included then the sample might not account for variation in the different types of news texts. A balanced news writing corpus would either include texts of sports, lifestyle, and general news texts or would select only one of these text types for analysis.

Table 5.1 below gives examples of projects and the type of corpora that would need to be built to address specific research topics. Notice that some of the corpora consist of sub-corpora that are investigated separately in order to determine possible variation. Corpora looking at gender differences in song lyrics, fitness articles, or romance novels include sub-corpora of texts written by or intended for different gender identities. The same sub-corpora approach is also seen in projects that investigate language variation in blog posts by Christians and Atheists and news talk shows from different political perspectives or newspaper articles written in different countries. Other types of corpora do not have sub-corpora attached to them. For example, a project that compares the language of Facebook posts to different registers would compare the linguistic features of the "Facebook Corpus" with different registers of use in existing corpora.

Once you have located relevant texts that can be used to build a balanced specialized corpus, you will need to prepare the text to be read by a software program such as AntConc, a popular and powerful program available free of charge. Different types of texts have different types of character encoding associated with them. If you use texts from the internet, the texts will likely be in Hypertext Mark-Up Language (HTML). A text that is read on a web browser such as Google Chrome or Safari looks like this:

You are not very good at parking. You're just not. Unless you happen to be a middle-aged gentleman from China called Han Yue. If you are indeed Mr Yue, then (a) welcome to TopGear.com, and (b) congratulations for obliterating the record for the tightest parallel park ... in the wooooorld. Again.

(Top Gear, 2014)

Table 5.1 Examples of corpus projects

Project	Type of corpus
Gender identity and song lyrics	Song lyrics written by people with different gender identities
News writing vs. news talk	A news corpus consisting of both written news and news talk shows
Gender and romance novel authors	A corpus of romance novels written by men and women
Gender differences in fitness articles	A corpus of fitness articles written by men and by women
Variation in English: Newspaper language in the United States and in China	A corpus of English newspaper articles written in the United States and in China (in English)
Language differences in religious and non-religious blogs	A corpus of blogs written by Christians and Atheists
Simplification of daily news reports for the ESL learner	A corpus of newspaper articles written for the general public and for second language learners of English
Comparison of language in Pakistani, British, and American newspaper English	A corpus of newspaper articles in American, British, and Pakistani English
Linguistic bias in the media	A corpus of news talk shows by left and right leaning hosts

If this file were to be a part of your corpus and you were to save this text in an HTML format, the HTML code would be a part of the text and would include information related to web and text design that is not seen in the text. The text that is not part of the actual text to be examined is often called "meta-text", and it is typically put in between brackets < ... >. The file would look something like this:

<p><span style="background-color: #888888;">You are not very good at parking. You're just not. Unless you happen to be a middle-aged gentleman from China called Han Yue. If you are indeed Mr Yue, then (a) welcome to TopGear.com, and (b) congratulations for obliterating the record for the tightest parallel park ... in the wooooorld. Again.</span></p><p><spanstyle="background-color:#888888;"> <source>(source:www.topgear.com/uk/car-news/parking-world-record-video-2014–20–11)</span></p>

As you can see from the HTML example above, in addition to the actual text information in the file, there is also extra material that is not relevant to the text to be analyzed. A similar type of extra information is also present in other types of files, such as Microsoft Word documents. In order to take this superfluous information out of the text, you will need to convert any text that you collect into a text file (a file with the extension ".txt"). The ".txt" format removes all of the mark-up language found in many other file extensions and allows a software program such as AntConc to find textual patterns instead of other patterns related to format or font type. There are different ways you can convert a file into a text file. If you are collecting texts from the internet, you can cut and paste each text into a text file and then use the "save as" option in order to ensure the file is saved in a plain text format. This same method works if you have a Microsoft Word document. If you are dealing with many texts, saving each file into a different format can be tedious and time-consuming. Alternatively, there are a number of online file conversion programs available free of charge such as AntConverter. These programs will allow you to convert multiple HTML/doc/docx, or.pdf files into.txt files using a simple conversion program.

A final and very important aspect of corpus building involves naming and saving your files so you are able to identify and retrieve them. To return to the fictitious news writing corpus project described above, a corpus used to analyze this issue may have 600 total texts, with 200 from three different time periods. For the purposes of analysis, you would want to have the 200 texts available as sub-corpora so you could load each of the sub-corpora separately to see if the files in one sub-corpora varied from those in another. This would mean that you would need to know which file goes with which sub-corpora. Devising a coding scheme will allow you to clearly identify each text as a separate text but also as part of a larger group of texts. As a simple example, a coding scheme could use a six-number system in which the first two numbers provide information on the time period of the text and the last four numbers provide the number of the text in each time period.

This coding scheme would allow you to clearly identify the text with "010001" being the first text in time period A, "010002" being the second text in time period A, and so on. In order to ensure that the text numbers relate to the characteristics of each text, each text will also have the relevant header information described above. Note that this entire corpus – let us call it A Historical Corpus of American News Writing – would consist of three sub-corpora related to each of the three time periods. All of the files in a single time period would be available in a single folder so that each sub-corpus could be loaded separately. Depending on different research

Table 5.2 Coding scheme

Sub corpus	Text number
Time period A: 01	0001
Time period B: 02	0001
Time period C: 03	0001

questions, the corpus could also be loaded with all three time periods. Note that if the files followed a consistent labeling practice, you would be able to determine the time periods by reference to the file name easily.

An alternative way to name files would be to use transparent file names with "word strings" instead of numbers. This way, the file names are transparent immediately, and information about the extra-textual features of the files can be accessed easily. If you choose to do this, you will need to make sure that the filename length is the same even though you may not have information in a particular category (for easier processing). For example, "news_15_election_00" would mean a news text from 2015 about an election in 2000.

Depending on your research goal and the design of your corpus, you may also want to include specific information on the situational characteristics of each text in individual text files in your corpus. Specific information such as the length of each text (by number of words), the topic, or the type of each text (if you included different types within a specific genre) can also be included in individual text files. This type of information is not a part of the text analysis but it can provide important interpretive information used in the functional analysis of your results. In a corpus of general song lyrics, you would want to include lyrics from different types of music (rock, rap, country, popular music, etc.) in order to achieve balance in your corpus. To be able to identify these different types of song lyrics, you could either come up with a system of naming each file (as described above) or you could include some of this information in each text file. Because you do not want this information counted as part of the linguistic characteristics of your text, you can put this or any other relevant information that you do not want to be a part of the linguistic analysis into angled brackets (< >). This type of information is included in the "headers" of the text but will not be read by the concordance software. Thus, each individual text file can include a relevant header and other extra-textual information as well as the text itself.

Figure 5.1 below is taken from a corpus of argumentative writing by university students who do not speak English as a first language. There are six different headers that specify (in order): 1) gender; 2) age; 3) native language; 4) degree program; 5) location of university; and 6) topic of essay. In order to ensure that the header information is not included in the text analysis, the software program needs to know that information in the angled brackets should be ignored in the text analysis. This can be achieved by indicating that all information in the angled brackets should be considered extra information, or "tags". An example of this is provided for AntConc (see more on this in the next section) as seen in Figure 5.2 below. The left bracket is identified as the start of the tag information and the right bracket is used as the end of the tagged information. This essentially

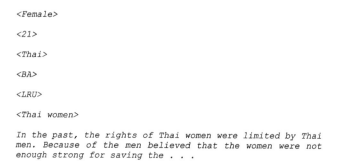

```
<Female>

<21>

<Thai>

<BA>

<LRU>

<Thai women>

In the past, the rights of Thai women were limited by Thai
men. Because of the men believed that the women were not
enough strong for saving the . . .
```

Figure 5.1 Example of a text file with header information

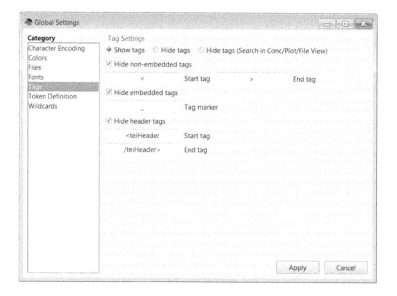

Figure 5.2 Embedding header tags in AntConc

tells the software program to ignore all the information that is included between the brackets as it does the textual processing and analysis.

However you go about constructing your corpus, you should use the following questions to guide the process:

1. Do the texts in my corpus allow for an investigation of a specific research issue?
2. Is the corpus constructed in a balanced manner?
3. Are the texts in a file format that will allow for analysis by the corpus software you will use in your analysis?

4. Does each text have a specific code and/or header information so that specific information in each file is identifiable?
5. If relevant to your research goal, is the corpus constructed so that specific sub-corpora are readily retrievable?

5.4 Software Programs and Your Corpus

As we mentioned in previous chapters, Laurence Anthony works at Waseda University in Japan (www.laurenceanthony.net/software.html). He develops software programs that are extremely useful for corpus linguistic analyses and he makes them freely available (although you are able to make a donation should you choose to do so). To date, there are 17 software programs available for PCs, Macs, and LINUX. While it is worth finding out about each one of the programs on Anthony's webpage as they are very useful, we will mainly focus on two here, AntWordProfiler for lexical analyses and AntConc for lexical as well as grammatical analyses, as the most pertinent for your use when analyzing your corpus.

5.4.1 AntWordProfiler

The function of Anthony's word profiler is very similar to what we saw with WordandPhrase, except for two main differences: 1) You can use as many texts as you want at once for an analysis; and 2) instead of using COCA as the background or monitor corpus, this one uses two other word lists (General Service List by Michael West, 1953, and Nation's academic word list) on which vocabulary frequency bands are based. (See Figure 5.3.)

Download the "Help" file from www.laurenceanthony.net/software/antwordprofiler/releases/AntWordProfiler141/help.pdf. After reading it, answer the following questions:

1. What kind of information can you get to know about your text(s) through the Vocabulary Profile Tool?
2. What kind of activities can you do through the File Viewer and Editor tool?
3. What do the different menu options do?

Project 5.1: Vocabulary Comparison

Let's say you are interested in finding out about the differences in the way vocabulary is used in a Wikipedia page and your own term paper on the same topic. Take one of the papers that you have written for another class and save it as a text file. Then search for the same topical area on Wikipedia, and copy the text, saving it into a text file. Read both texts into the AntWord Profiler, and run the program twice, once on each individual file.

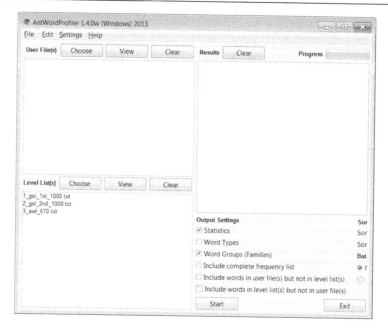

Figure 5.3 AntConc using three-word lists for vocabulary frequency comparison

Note the differences you see between your text and the Wikipedia text in the following areas:[1]

a. Number of lines
b. Number of word types
c. Number of word tokens
d. Number of word tokens that fall into each of the three vocabulary bands
e. Percentage of word coverage from the various vocabulary bands

If you remember, at the WordandPhrase site, each text was marked with a different color depending on the frequency band it belonged to. Can we achieve that kind of marking with this tool? If so, how? Would you modify your text to use less or more frequent words? In what situation(s) do you think modifying words in a text this way could be a useful tool? What other kinds of information can you obtain through this tool?

5.4.2 AntConc

The function of Anthony's concordance program is similar to what we saw at the main interface of COCA. Using your own corpus, you should be able to do KWIC searches through the concordance lines, and other types of lexical as much as grammatical analyses in your own texts. Once again, download the "Help" file to get an overview of what is possible with this particular program (Anthony, 2023).

Clearly, this program is capable of facilitating some of the same kinds of analyses COCA did but with your own texts. Among those analyses are: KWIC (keyword in context), n-grams, collocates in a particular text, and word lists. In addition, this program is able to show you how the word (or collocate or lexical bundle or any n-gram) is distributed within each of your texts (a concordance plot) as well as how many texts include examples of your search term.

Read in (i.e., upload) your corpus through the "File" menu ("Open files") and type any search word in the search box that you would like to find out about in your text(s) and hit the "start" button to get a KWIC concordance line. (See Figure 5.4.)

If you press the "Sort" button, the words following the search term will be in alphabetical order. It is important to keep in mind that the colors in AntConc do not denote part of speech categories as they do in COCA; they simply show first and second and third place after the search term. (See Figure 5.5.)

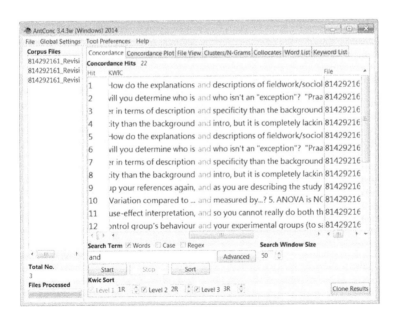

Figure 5.4 Searching your own corpus: Concordance lines in AntConc for the word "and"

If you click on the word in the concordance lines, it will show you the larger textual window (see Figure 5.6).

As mentioned above, if you click on the "Concordance plot" tab, you will get a view of the spread of your search term in each of the files you uploaded as part of your corpus (see Figure 5.7).

It is also possible to identify collocates of your search term. In Figure 5.8, we specified that the collocate that we are looking for should come either one word to the right or one word to the left of the keyword specified in the window-span at the bottom.

If you click on any word on the list, it will bring you to a concordance line listing the instances of that collocate; by clicking on the word, you can take it from here for a larger textual span, as you have seen above. (See Figure 5.9.)

You can also generate an n-gram list based on the texts you have. Click on the "Clusters/N-grams" tab on the top and click on "N-grams" under the search term on the bottom, and also specify how big the window size should be under "N-gram size". If you are interested in lexical bundles, you should also specify what the minimum cut-off is under "minimum frequency" and "minimum range" just below. In Figure 5.10, we set the n-gram size anywhere between two and four words, and the minimum frequency at ten.

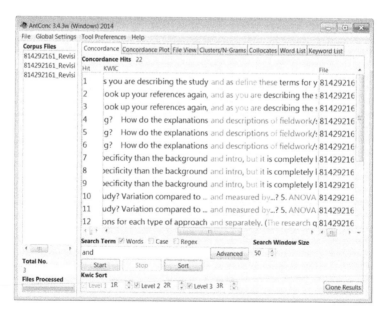

Figure 5.5 Sorting in AntConc

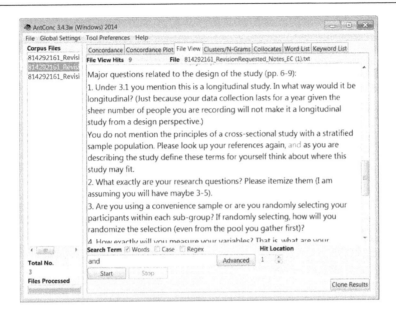

Figure 5.6 File view in AntConc

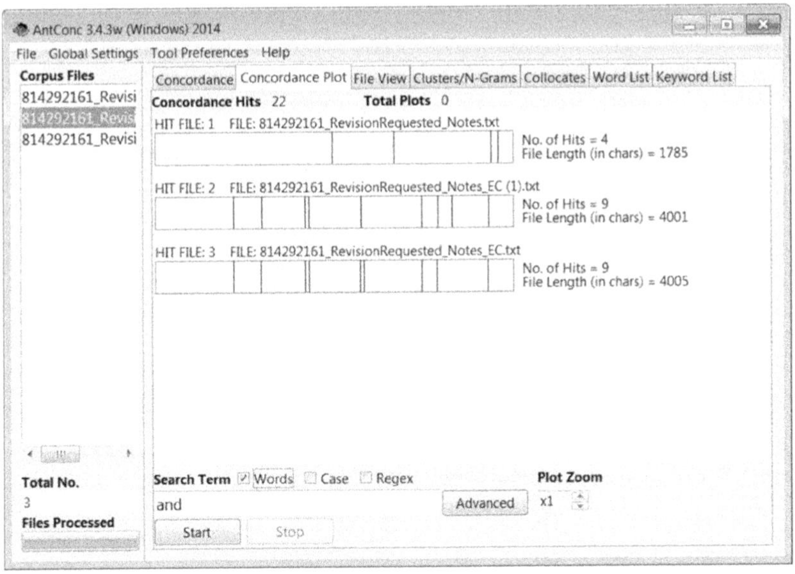

Figure 5.7 Search term distribution in full texts

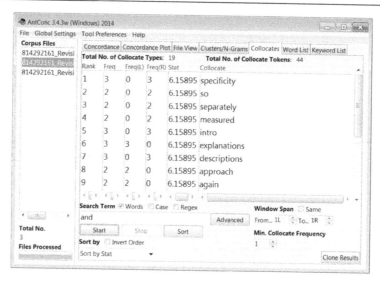

Figure 5.8 The word "and" and its collocates

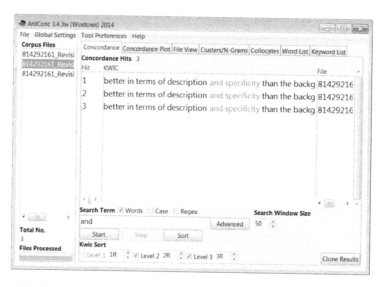

Figure 5.9 Collocates in concordance lines

Finally, you can also generate simple word lists with frequency counts and rankings from your own dataset (Figure 5.11).

When you finish your analysis, be sure to clear all your files and tools, unless you want to reuse them when you open the program again.

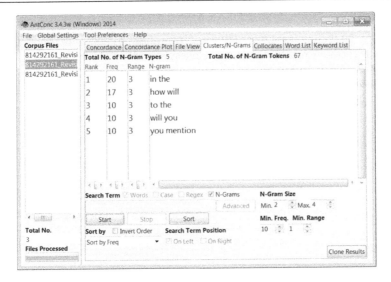

Figure 5.10 Running your own n-grams in AntConc

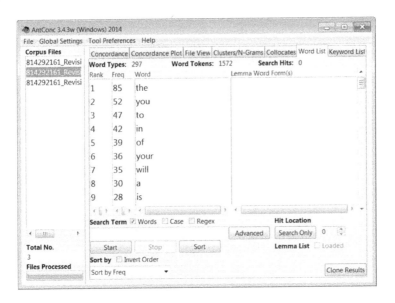

Figure 5.11 Running a word list in your corpus in AntConc

Note

1 Word tokens are each word in a text, while word types are each type of word in a text. For example, in the following text (two sentences), there are eight tokens (eight-word tokens) and six word types (*the* and *cat* are repeated, so they count as one type each): *He saw the cat. The cat was black.*

References

Anthony, L. (2023). AntConc (Windows, Macintosh OS X, and Linux) www.laurenceanthony.net/software/antconc/releases/AntConc343/help.pdf

Top Gear (2014, November 20). www.topgear.com/uk/car-news/parking-world-record-video-2014-20-11

Chapter 6

Basic Statistics

6.1 Why Do Statistical Analyses?

When doing register analyses, researchers look for patterns of language use and their associations with the texts' situational characteristics. We need empirical measures to see what these associations are, and we need quantitative measures (e.g., the frequency of a particular language feature) to see how commonly these patterns occur. We can then look at how the frequency of that measure is distributed across the two or more situations that we are interested in.

Descriptive statistics will give us averages through which we can compare typical uses of the features in question. However, this only gives us an impressionistic view of the difference for our dataset. If we rely solely on descriptive statistics, we cannot tell how generalizable those differences may be. To be able to generalize about the "typicality" of patterns of use, we need to use other statistical procedures.

Generalizability means that the results in our sample can be predicted to be true, with a high level of certainty, to samples outside of our own dataset as well. That is, if we were to conduct a new study under the same conditions we are reporting on, we could be 95% or 99% certain to get the same results. In order to have generalizable results, we need to make sure that a set of assumptions about our data is met (see later in this chapter).

6.2 Basic Terms, Concepts, and Assumptions

In this section, we outline the basic terms and concepts that are used when doing any kind of statistical analysis. First, we discuss variable types and

DOI: 10.4324/9781003363309-9

levels that are critical to know before any test can be done. Second, we introduce measures of central tendency ("typicality" in a dataset) and measures of variability or dispersion ("spread").

6.2.1 Variables and Observations

Variables are typically classified based on a) the type of variable and how they function in the research design, and b) the range of values and levels they can have. It is crucial to think about this ahead of time because the validity and reliability of our research depends on how we define our variables and observations. Also, the variable scale and type determines the types of statistical analyses that can be done.

Variable Types and Functions

"Regular variables" are variables that you either manipulate or want to see change in your design. They can have a range of values (numeric) or levels (non-numeric). Numeric values are relevant if you have frequencies of a linguistic feature (e.g., the number of personal pronouns in a text). Non-numeric values (or levels) are relevant when you refer to a variable in terms of categories, e.g., class size ("small" or "large"). Instead of calling them small or large, you could also give numbers to these categories (e.g., small = 1 and large = 2); however, they are not values, just numeric codes. That is, there is nothing inherently primary or secondary in the number they are assigned to.

Further classification of regular variables is based on the function they have in the design. We distinguish between two types: dependent variables and independent variables. Dependent variables are the variables that you are most interested in for your research because you think that the values of the variable (e.g., frequency) will change (or not) as you are manipulating some external factors around it. The change that will occur (or not) depends on your manipulation of other variables around it. Independent variables are the variables that you manipulate in order to see whether there is a change in the dependent variable. Dependent variables are often called "outcomes" and independent variables are often called "predictors" (of change).

EXAMPLE

You read in an educational journal article that lectures in small classes are more "personable" than in large classes. As there is no linguistic evidence provided in the article for this claim, you want to find out yourself. You decide that you will use first person pronouns (*I, we*) as a measure of "personable". You are interested in whether the frequency of first person pronouns (*I*, *we* – and all their variants) changes at all when you are attending a lecture in a large class with 200 students or in a small, seminar-like class with 20 students. You hope to see that the frequency of first person pronouns will change depending on which class you attend. That is, the use of first person pronouns will depend on the class size (lecture versus seminar-type). The dependent variable in this design is first person pronouns (the frequency of which will change) and the independent variable is class size (the one that you manipulate to see the change). So, your predictor for change in the outcome (pronoun use) is class size.

"Moderator variables" are referred to as other predictors or other independent variables in your design (if you have more than one). Moderator variables are viewed as independent variables potentially interacting with other independent variables. In our example, let's say you want to see whether the instructor's gender also has an effect on the use of first person pronouns in small or large classes. Your independent variable is class size and the moderator (or other independent variable) is gender. In this design, you may be interested in whether it really is class size alone, or gender alone, or the two independent variables together (class size moderated by gender) that cause a change in the use of first person pronouns.

"Control variables" are not real variables in the way we have been describing variables so far. You are not able to measure a control variable in your study; instead, it is just something you control for.

"Intervening variables" are variables that you should have measured in your study but you realize later that you didn't. Typically, these are the variables that are mentioned in the discussion section of an article or report when calling for further research.

Variable Scales

"Nominal scales" (also called categorical, discrete, discontinuous scales) are variables measuring categories. They are used in naming and categorizing data in a variable, usually in the form of identity groups, or memberships. The variable could occur naturally (e.g., sex, nationality) or artificially (experimental, control groups), or any other way, but in all cases, it is a limited number of categories. They represent non-numeric categories (e.g., religion, L1, ethnicity). When they are assigned to numbers, they carry no numeric value. Instead, they are only a category identifier (e.g., there are two sexes: 1 = male, and 2 = female).

"Ordinal scales" are used to order or rank data. There is no fixed interval, or numeric relationship in the data other than one is "greater than" or "lesser than" the other. No fixed interval means that we don't know whether the difference between 1 and 2 is the same as between 4 and 5 (i.e., no fixed interval between values as is the case for interval scales).

Examples of ordinal scales are holistic scoring, Likert scales, and question-naires. They are numeric in that the numbers represent one being more – or less – than the other, but they do not say how much more.

"Interval scales" reflect the interval or distance between points of rank-ing. They are numeric, continuous scales, and are the same as ordinal but with fixed intervals. That is, while with ordinal scales we do not know whether the difference between 2 and 3 is the same as between 4 and 5, with interval scales we do. For example, the difference between 18 and 19 milliseconds is the same as between 22 and 23 – that is, one millisecond. The difference between 2 and 3 meters is the same as between 4 and 5 meters – that is, one meter, 100 centimeters, 1,000 millimeters (no matter how we measure it, the difference is exactly the same). This means that we always know how much more or less distance there is between the two measures. Sometimes, frequencies, test grades, or evaluation are considered interval variables; however, it is not really fixed. The best way to deal with frequencies, for instance, is to put them under a scale, at which point they become interval scores. We can do this by norming[1] frequency counts, for example, or by calculating percentages.

"Ratio" only tells us about the relationship between two measures. It is not a very good measure for register studies. Let's say we want to compare two texts to see which one has more nouns.

> Text 1: noun/verb ratio =.27
> Text 2: noun/verb ratio =.32

We are unable to tell which text has more nouns because it is only in rela-tion to the verbs that we might have more nouns. That is, ratios measure how common one thing is but only in relation to a potentially unrelated other thing.

Variable Values (Levels)

Variables can have multiple values or levels. For example, if participant age is a variable, the (numerical) values can be counted between 0 and 120. If ethnicity is a variable, we can list what ethnicities we would want to in-clude and give each a nominal value. For example, African American = 1, Native American = 2, Asian American = 3, etc.

Observations

Observations are individual objects that you are characterizing. They pro-vide the unit of analysis that will make up your data. For register studies, an observation is typically each text that you enter into your database.

For other linguistic studies, it could be the individual linguistic feature you are considering or the individual test-taker whose language you are characterizing.

EXAMPLE

Let's assume you are interested in how complement clauses are used by younger and older generations and also how they are used by people with different educational backgrounds. You are using a corpus to look for patterns. Take 100 instances of complement clauses and mark each for who uses them in terms of age and educational background (hopefully, this information will be available in the corpus). You can use other contextual variables as well, but the focus should be on the two variables you identified. Instead of listing your findings in a table exemplified by Table 6.1, you list the individual cases in a table exemplified in Table 6.2.

Table 6.2 is preferable because, given the way the information is presented in Table 6.1, we are unable to distinguish between the two variables. That is, we cannot measure one independent variable from another. Variables are confounded when the variables measure the same thing; that is, based on the data in Table 6.1, we can't say whether the frequency of complements is due to age or level of education.

6.2.2 Measures of Central Tendency and Measures of Variability

Central tendency describes typical values for a variable; that is, it is the central point in the distribution of values in the data. Dispersion, on the other hand, is how much variation you get within your data. Both of these are important measures to see patterns.

Measures of Central Tendency

Measures of central tendency tell us about the most typical score for a dataset. There are three types: mode, median, and mean.

"Mode" works for any variable scale (nominal, ordinal, or interval). It is the most frequent/common value (whatever value occurs with highest

Table 6.1 Frequency of complement clauses

	18–22	22–30	31–40	41+
Undergrad	50	10	2	2
MA	5	20	10	10
PhD	0	3	20	3

Table 6.2 Complement clauses

Clause	Complement type	Age	Education
I told her that he likes me	Verb	20	BA
I like the idea that we go by boat	Noun	30	MA
The claim that he was happy turned out to be untrue	Noun	30	PhD

frequency) in your dataset. If you draw a frequency polygon, it will show the most frequently occurring point best. For example, in the following dataset, what would be the mode?

2, 2, 3, 3, 3, 3, 3, 3, 4, 4, 5

Yes, the mode is 3, because that is the score that occurs most frequently (six times), versus 2 (twice), 4 (twice), and 5 (once).

There are, however, problems with using mode as a measure of central tendency, namely:

- If there is not one most frequent score (but more than one – for instance, two, just like two and four above occur with the same frequency, so if those two were the most frequent scores, we could not tell what the mode is), there is no mode.
- If each ranked score in the dataset only occurs once, i.e., no score receives a frequency higher than one (i.e., every score in the dataset occurs just once), there is no mode.
- The mode is too sensitive to chance scores (when a mistake is made in entering the scores).

"Median" works for any numeric variable (ordinal or interval). It is the 50th percentile (i.e., the middle observation). To calculate the median, rank order all scores and the observation in the middle is the median. If you have an even number of scores, the median will be in between the two middle scores; if you have an odd number of scores, the median is the middle score. The quartiles are located as well in the ranking, and the number of observations that go with each score with the same number of observations from both sides. Let's say we have the average scores for the use of hedges in our corpus of nine texts.

17   18 | 19   20   20   20   21 | 22   23

25th   50th   75th

The quartile gives us distributional patterns in the data. In this example, the 25th percentile means that 25% of the texts display a score of 18.5 or less; the 50th percentile means that half of the texts display a score of 20 or more and half of the texts display a score of 20 or less, and finally, the 75th percentile means that 75% of the texts display a score of 21.5 or less.

Median is often used as a measure of central tendency when:

- the number of scores is relatively small
- the data have been obtained by rank order measurement (e.g., a Likert scale)
- the mean is not appropriate (because the variable is not interval – see below)

Boxplots are typically used as visuals to show the range of scores (minimum and maximum), the 25th, the 50th (median), and the 75th percentile. A boxplot is also able to show outliers in the dataset. In the example below, we display the use of nouns by teachers and students in the corpus.

25th percentile (on box plot: lowest line where the box starts)
50th percentile (median – on box plot: thick black line in box)
75th percentile (on box plot: highest line where the box finishes)

The range, the percentile figures, and the outlier are in Figure 6.1. Boxplots do not tell you the individual scores.

"Mean" (x bar) only works for interval scale. Add up all the values (x) and divide by the # of cases or observations (N) to get the arithmetic average of all scores.

$$\bar{X} = \frac{\sum x}{N}$$

X (X bar) = sum of x divided by N

While the mean is the best measure of central tendency for interval scores, it is at times problematic because it is too sensitive to extreme scores. If extreme scores enter the equation, it throws the mean off so much that it cannot be the measure of tendency anymore.

EXAMPLE

Let's say you are interested in finding out whether undergraduate students majoring in natural sciences use fewer "hedges" (*sort of*, *kind* of) than

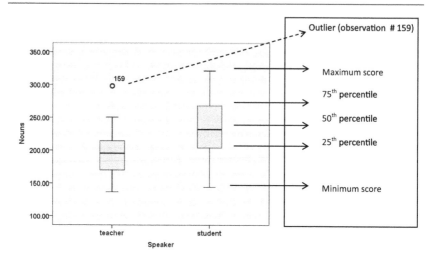

Figure 6.1 Boxplot of the use of nouns by teachers and students

students in the humanities or in the social sciences. You look at a corpus of student presentations that includes nine presentations from each area. The data below shows the mean scores for each of the presenters in each of the three areas. It illustrates how much one score in the dataset can change the value of the mean, which is the measure of central tendency.

In Group A, you have the mean scores for social science students.
A: 0   1   2   20   20   20   97   98   99
Group A results Mode: 20; Median: 20; Mean: 39.6 (357/9)
In Group B, the mean scores are listed for natural sciences students.
B: 17   18   19   20   20   20   21   22   23
Group B results Mode: 20; Median: 20; Mean: 20 (180/9)
Group C contains the mean scores for humanities students.
C: 17   18   19   20   20   20   21   22   99
Group C results Mode: 20; Median: 20; Mean: 28.4 (256/9)

As you can see, the mode (most frequent scores) and median (the central score after rank ordering all scores) are the same for all three groups. However, the mean becomes vastly different depending on the actual scores in the dataset. In Group A, the scores vary a great deal. Social sciences students use hedges in an idiosyncratic way; that is, it really depends on the individual. Some students use none or very few, and some use a lot! When this is true, the mean is relatively high (especially in comparison with the others). In Group B, the scores are not going into extremes. Instead, they are pretty evenly distributed. That is, the students in this group more or less use hedges the same way, or at least very similarly. In Group C, students overall use hedges similarly but there is one student who hedges a lot. That one student changes the mean score dramatically. The two scores in Groups B and C are very different (20 in Group B and 28.4 in Group C) and that difference is due to only one score. In the mean score, one outlier makes a big difference.

The characteristic of a normal distribution is that the mode, the median, and the mean are identical. Group B above has that example. And if you look at the variability of the scores, you can see that it is steadily in order. There are no outliers or extreme scores in the dataset. The scores are simply normally distributed.

Measures of Variability and Dispersion

Measures of variability and dispersion only work with interval scale type data. While range looks at the scores at each end of the distribution, variance and standard deviation measures look at the distance of every score from the mean and average them. More specifically, range only takes the highest and the lowest scores into the computation, and variance and standard deviation take each score into account.

"Range" tells us the spread of scores. We compute the range by subtracting the lowest score from the highest score.

$$Range = x_{highest} - x_{lowest}$$

For example, the range of scores for Group A in the example above is 99, for Group B it is 6, and for Group C it is 82. The problem here is the same as with the mean scores, as it changes drastically when you have more extreme scores (as you see in the examples). Since it is unstable, it is rarely used for statistical reporting, but calculating the range could be informative as a piece of additional information (e.g., to see whether there is an outlier).

"Quartile" (interquartile) or percentile measures tell us how the scores are spread in different intervals in the dataset. As outlined above, the median is a measure of central tendency, and by adding the interquartile figures (the percentile figures), we are able to see the spread as well. Once again, the 25th percentile tells us what scores we would get for a quarter of our data, the 50th percentile tells us what score we would get for half of the data and the 75th percentile refers to the score we would get for three-quarters of the data.

"Variance" summarizes the distance (i.e., how far) individual scores are from the mean. Let's say our mean is 93.5 ($\bar{X}$ = 93.5). If we have a score of 89 (x = 89), that means our score is 4.5 points away from the mean, and that is the deviation (value) away from the mean. In this instance, we just discussed one score only. However, what we want is a measure that takes the distribution and deviation of all scores in the dataset into account. This is the variance.

To compute variance, take the deviation of the individual scores from the mean, square each deviation, add them up (oftentimes called the "sum of squares") and average them for the dataset dividing it by the number of observations minus one. As a formula, it looks like this:

$$variance = \frac{\Sigma\left(x_{individual\ score} - \bar{X}_{group\ mean}\right)^2}{N-1}$$

"Standard deviation" is a measure of variability in the data from the point of central tendency. Standard deviation tells us the variability of the scores – i.e., the spread of the scores from the central point – and is most often used as a measure of dispersion in studies of a variety of fields, including corpus linguistic studies. But why is this important? Let's take an example that illustrates why it is important to know the spread. With another example, from Csomay (2002), we can illustrate how the mean score is not enough to know in order to determine the distribution of scores, while the dispersion measure would tell us the answer to that question.

EXAMPLE

Imagine you would like to find out whether one class is more interactive than another. As Csomay (2002) did, you define interactivity by the number of turns taken in a class and by how long those turns are (in terms of number of words). You look at two lecture segments to compare. Each has five turns, and for simplicity, each segment has a total of 150 words in them. Here are the numbers:

Lecture #1: 5 turns, a total of 150 words, average turn length 30 words, each turn is of equal length.
Turn 1: 30 words
Turn 2: 30 words
Turn 3: 30 words

Turn 4: 30 words
Turn 5: 30 words
Total = 5 turns, 150 words
Average turn length: 30

$$\bar{X} = 30$$

Lecture #2: 5 turns, a total of 150 words, average turn length 30 words, turn length varies for each turn.
Turn 1: 2 words
Turn 2: 140 words
Turn 3: 2 words
Turn 4: 3 words
Turn 5: 3 words
Total = 5 turns, 150 words
Average turn length: 30

$$\bar{X} = 30$$

In both instances, the average (mean) turn length is 30 words, which is the measure of central tendency. But it is clear that one lecture is very different from another in terms of turn length measures. By calculating the standard deviation for each, we are able to tell the spread in the scores; that is, whether the scores are close to each other or they vary, and if the latter, how much they vary (in terms of magnitude measured by a single number). For Lecture #1, the standard deviation is 0, and for Lecture #2, it is 61.49. A zero standard deviation says that there is no variation in the scores at all (clearly), and 61.49, being very high, tells us that there is a great variation in the scores.

Does this tell us which lecture is more interactive? If we think that relatively shorter turns are making the class more interactive, then Lecture #1 is more interactive. If we think that longer stretches of turns coupled with two- or three-word turns is more interactive, then Lecture #2 it is. Lecture #1 looks to be the best candidate simply because the number of turns and the turn length measure together tell us that people would have more opportunity to express actual ideas rather than just agree to what is happening with one or two words at a time (see Csomay, 2012 for short turn content).

In sum, the larger the standard deviation, the wider the distribution of scores is away from the measure of central tendency (the mean). The smaller the standard deviation, the more similar the scores are, and the more tightly the values are clustered around the mean.

To calculate the standard deviation, all you need to do is to square root the variance (explained above).

standard deviation = $\sqrt{variance}$.

that is,

$$sd = \sqrt{\frac{\sum \left(x_{individual\ score} - \bar{X}_{group\ mean} \right)^2}{N-1}}$$

For the scores above in Lecture #2, it would look like this:

2–30 = –28 squared: 784
140 – 30 = 110 squared: 12,100
2–30 = –28 squared: 784
3–30= –27 squared: 729
3–30= –27 squared: 729

Sum: 15,126 divided by $N - 1$ (5 – 1 = 4) = 3,781.5 square root: 61.49

With this, we are able to see that two groups could be very similar in terms of their means but they can be very different because the distribution of scores away from the mean may be quite different.

6.2.3 Parametric and Non-Parametric Tests, Research Questions, and Hypotheses

Parametric and Non-Parametric Tests

Non-parametric tests do not require strong assumptions about the distribution of the data. The observations can be frequencies (nominal scores) or ordinal scales and can be rank-ordered. They can be used with interval scales, too, when we are unable to meet the assumptions of parametric tests (e.g., normal distribution in the data). Non-parametric test results can only be interpreted in relation to the dataset in question. That is, no projections or predictions could be made about the population it was drawn from, and the interpretation can only relate to the dataset investigated. A non-parametric test, for example, is Chi-square (see details on this in Chapter 7).

Parametric tests, however, do require strong assumptions about the nature and the distribution of the data. These assumptions are:

1. Dependent variables are interval scales (where means and standard deviations are the measures of central tendency and dispersion,

respectively) and not frequencies or ordinal data. If you are using corpus data from COCA, for example, you may not want to use the frequency data but the normed score (frequency per million words) to make sure your values are interval.

2. Dependent variables are strongly continuous (rather than discrete as ordinal scores are). That is, we know exactly how much difference there is between two scores and they are always at the same distance.

3. We can estimate the distribution in the population from which the respective samples are taken. That is, the distribution in the "sample" could be projected to the distribution of the "population". A small sample size will make it problematic to do this – a minimum of 30 observations for each variable is needed. If you compare two registers, for example, you will need values for your dependent variable from at least 30 texts (observations) for each register.

4. Data are normally distributed (sometimes we use fewer than 30 observations – remember that is the minimum to assume normality in the distribution – the larger the size, the better, of course).

5. Observations are independent; otherwise, research is confounded, as discussed before – that is, there is no relationship between the observations, or cases.

Why do parametric tests? The reason parametric tests are more powerful than non-parametric tests is because a) they have predictive power (i.e., we can predict that if we followed the same procedures, and did the study the same way, we will gain the same results) and therefore, b) the results are generalizable (i.e., we can generalize that the results are true to the larger population the samples are drawn from – that is, if we repeat the study with the same parameters, we would get the same results). Therefore, they are very powerful!

Research Questions and Hypotheses

According to Hatch and Lazaraton (1991), the characteristics of research questions are:

(a) Keywords to define the area
(b) Element of new information
(c) Manageable data
(d) Question that is specific enough to make the study focused

Research questions have three components:

(a) What group are you dealing with? What collection of things (not only people)?

(b) What happens? What are the outcomes? What result are you looking for?
(c) What influences the results?

Hypotheses, on the other hand, are basically the formalization of research questions into strict statements that could be rejected (or not):

(a) They are phrased in the form of statements (rather than questions).
(b) Their statements show specific outcomes.
(c) They need to be testable.

In other words, a "hypothesis is a statement of possible outcome of research" (Hatch & Lazaraton, 1991: 24). We have a null hypothesis and alternative hypotheses. The null hypothesis (H_0) is a statement – usually a negative statement, and the alternative hypothesis is the opposite, a positive statement. Additionally, the alternative hypothesis then could be in a directional form, taking a (+/–) direction. Our aim is to reject the null hypothesis.

Typically, we are looking for either differences between two or more groups or we are looking for relationships between two groups (see Chapter 7 for further explanation).

In looking for differences, our null hypothesis will be stating that there is no difference between two or more groups (independent variables) with respect to some measure (dependent variable). (These are typically parametric tests.)

For example, we may have the following null hypothesis:

H_0 There is no difference in the use of nouns across disciplines.

The alternative hypothesis would be:

H_1 There is a difference in the use of nouns across disciplines.

In looking for relationships between two or more variables our null hypothesis will be stating that there is no relationship between two or more measures.

H_0 There is no relationship between the use of nouns and first person pronouns in university classroom talk.

Alternative hypotheses:

H_1 There is a relationship between the use of nouns and first person pronouns in university classroom talk.

H_2 There is a positive relationship between the use of nouns and first person pronouns in university classroom talk. (That is, when nouns occur, first person pronouns will as well.)

H_3 There is a negative relationship between the use of nouns and first person pronouns in university classroom talk. (That is, when nouns occur, first person pronouns will not occur.)

We look to reject the null hypothesis of "no difference" or "no relationship". A $p < .05$ (probability of 5%) means that we have a 95% chance of being right in rejecting the null hypothesis. A $p < .01$ means that we have a 99% chance of being right in doing so, and a $p < .001$ means that we have a 99.9% chance of being right in rejecting the null hypothesis. There are two types of errors that we can commit in rejecting the hypothesis: Type 1 and Type 2. See their description below.

When we reject the null hypothesis, we want the probability (p) to be very low that we are wrong. If, on the other hand, we must accept the null hypothesis, we still want the probability to be very low that we are wrong in doing so.

(Hatch & Lazaraton, 1991: 224)

Type 1 error: The researcher rejects the hypothesis when it should not have been rejected.

Type 2 error: The researcher accepts the null hypothesis when it should have been rejected.

The probability value (alpha, or p) basically tells you how certain you can be that you are not committing a Type 1 error. When the probability level is very low ($p < .001$), we can feel confident that we are not committing a Type 1 error described above, and that our sample group of students differs from other groups who may have taken the test in the past or who might take it in the future (population). We test whether the data from that sample "fit" with that of the population. A $p < .05$ tells us that there are fewer than five chances in 100 that we are wrong in rejecting the H_0. That is, we can have confidence in rejecting the H_0.

Two-Tailed Test/Hypothesis

In two-tailed tests, we specify no direction for the null hypothesis ahead of time (that is, whether our scores will be higher or lower than more typical scores). We just say that they will not be different (and then reject that if significant). (See first example above.)

One-Tailed Test/Hypothesis

We have a good reason to believe that we will find a difference between the means based on previous findings. The one-tailed tests will specify the direction of the predicted difference. In a positive directional hypothesis, we expect the group to perform better than the population. (See second example above.) In a negative directional hypothesis, the sample group will perform worse than the population.

One crucial remark: We cannot repeat tests as often as we may want to. The statistical tests that we introduce in this book are not exploratory statistics, but they follow experimental designs, and test hypotheses. One-time deal only. Steps for hypothesis testing:

Step 1: State null hypothesis.
Step 2: Decide whether to test it as a one- or two-tailed hypothesis.
Question: Is there research evidence on the issue?

   a.   NO: Select two-tailed → will allow rejection of null hypothesis in favor of an alternative hypothesis.
   b.   YES: Select one-tailed → will allow rejection of null hypothesis in favor of directional.

Step 3: Set the probability level (typically $p < .05$ or lower). Justify your choice based on the literature.
Step 4: Select appropriate statistical test.
Step 5: Collect data – apply statistical test.
Step 6: Report the results and interpret them correctly.

6.3 How to Go About Getting the Statistical Results

Several statistical programs are commercially available and are potentially cheaper at a student price, and there are others that are free. While SAS, STATA, and R, for example, are powerful statistical software programs, we will be showing you how to do descriptive statistics and the basic statistical methods we outlined above with SPSS (Statistical Package for the Social Sciences). We consider this program the most user-friendly, as the other three mentioned above require some programming abilities. Also, SPSS is still the most frequently used program at university campuses and is typically available for the students at computer labs free of charge through a university license. In this section, we will show you how to organize your data in SPSS (very different from Excel!) and how to access descriptive statistical results.

6.3.1 Preparing the Data and Descriptive Statistics

In SPSS, the way we organize the data is very different from the way data could be entered in Excel. Therefore, we would like you to completely forget Excel while you are using SPSS. As a start, there are two views you can have in SPSS: the variable view and the data view. Before we explain each view a bit more in detail, let's review one more time the dependent versus independent variables and what the basic unit of analysis is (observations) in the example we use.

When we characterize registers based on one or more linguistic features, the unit of analysis is a text. That means that each observation is a text in which we look for the particular variable that we hope to see variation in (i.e., the dependent variable). In our examples, it has been an individual linguistic feature, such as nouns, or pronouns, etc. Each text then will have other, "extra-textual" features as well. An extra-textual feature is, for example, what register it comes from – that is, whether it is news, or face-to-face conversation, etc. Another extra-textual feature can be the time the text was produced: whether the text comes from the year 1920 or 2015. These are your independent variables, and depending on your research question, you will manipulate these to see if there is variation in the dependent variable.

When we characterize individual speakers' way of using certain language features, the unit of analysis is the text produced by those speakers. The unit of analysis is still the text (because the language was produced and transcribed), but it may not be obviously understood in the same sense as the text above because each text is more associated with individual speakers who would have certain characteristics. Yet, it is the text produced by them, and that will be the basis for comparison.

Finally, when we look at characteristics of individual linguistic features (e.g., article type in subject and object positions), our unit of analysis is each instance of that feature. Then, we characterize each observation for its features, which in this case would be syntactic position and type of article.

Preparing the Data: Entering Data into SPSS

We will now show you the basics in each view, and tell you how to organize your data in these two settings. Let's start with the variable view (see the highlighted tab at the bottom left-hand corner). Here, you will enter the names and characteristics of both your dependent and independent variables. Let's take the example we discussed earlier in this chapter when explaining the mean. Here's the text again: You are interested in finding out whether undergraduate students majoring in natural sciences use fewer "hedges" than students in the humanities or in the social sciences. You look at a corpus of student presentations that includes nine presentations from each area (a total of 27 texts). The data below shows the normed scores for "hedges" for each of the presenters in each of the three areas.

Social science presentations: 0   1   2   20   20   20   97   98   99
Natural sciences presentations: 17   18   19   20   20   20   21   22   23
Humanities presentations: 17   18   19   20   20   20   21   22   99

Your dependent variable is "hedges" (interval scores, as it is normed to, let's say, 1,000 words) and your independent variable is discipline (nominal) with three levels (the three disciplinary areas). Because SPSS is not good at processing "string" data, i.e., text, for its variables, we need to give a nominal numeric value to each discipline. We name Social Sciences 1, Natural Sciences 2, and Humanities 3. There is no numeric value across these categories.

Your SPSS Variable view will look like Figure 6.2.

We need to enter two variables in this view: one will be the dependent variable and the other will be the independent one. Remember, all variables

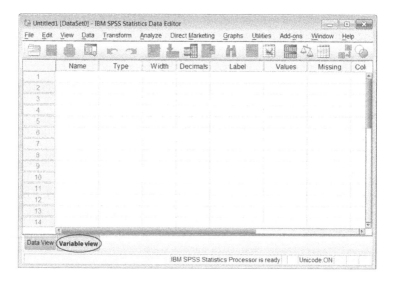

Figure 6.2 Variable view in SPSS

and their characteristics will need to be entered here. The names of the variables will be "hedge" and "discipline", respectively. So let's enter those and see what characteristics each has. (See Figure 6.3.)

We need to focus on some of these headings, but not all. For example, those that seem less important are "Width", which determines how wide the cell is in your data view, and "Columns", which determines how many columns there are. "Align" is also less important as it sets how you would like to see the text aligned in the data view (to the left, the middle, or to the right), and "Role" is what role you assign this variable in the dataset (it will all be input for us). We really do not need to worry much about these tabs. However, we do need to know more about all the others: "Type", "Decimals", "Label", "Values", "Missing", and "Measure". We will go through each of these one by one:

Type: Numeric (whether it has a numeric value or not – see nominal independent variables above).

Decimals: You can set the number of decimals you want to see. For interval scores, we typically use two decimal points and for nominal scores, we use zero decimal points (since they have no numeric value, they do not and will not have any fractions).

Label: SPSS takes very short names for variable names and only in one-word strings. Labels, then, provide you with the opportunity to give longer names that could be used as the labels for your output results as well.

Values: These are the values that you can assign to the levels. For hedges, we will not have any values assigned. But for the nominal variables, as we mentioned above, we have 1 = Social Sciences, 2 = Natural Sciences, and 3 = Humanities. As you enter each one, make sure you hit the "Add", or else it will not be added to the list. (See Figure 6.4.)

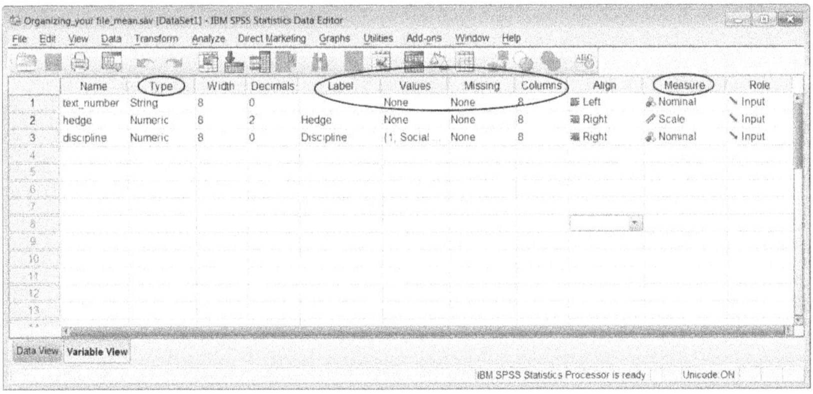

Figure 6.3 Important tabs in variable view in SPSS

Missing: It is good not to have any missing data because that will affect the calculations and the results or we need to set the software program in sophisticated ways not to do so.

Measure: In this area, you will need to determine what kind of variable you have. In our example, since hedges are interval variables, we will choose "Scale", and since discipline is a nominal variable, we will choose "Nominal". (See Figure 6.5.)

Before we turn to our data view, let's add one more variable, so we can keep track of our observations. The filenames will be portrayed as a string variable called "text_number" (we really are not including this as

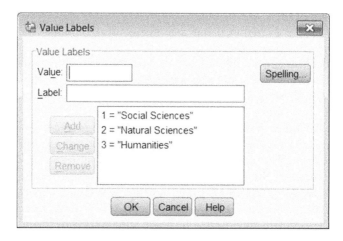

Figure 6.4 Value labels in SPSS

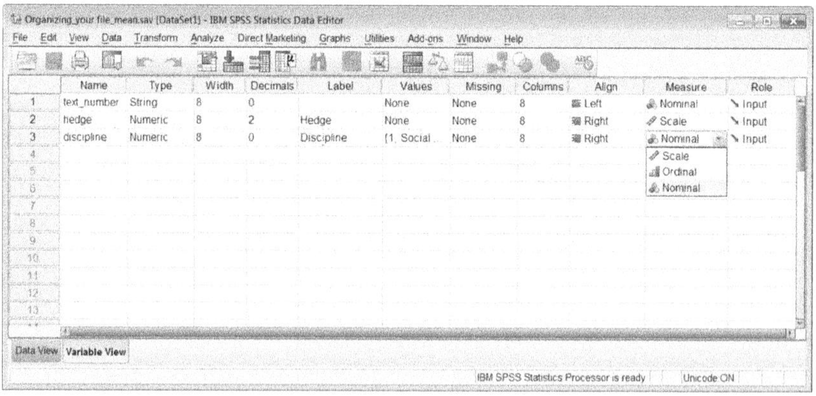

Figure 6.5 Measures in SPSS

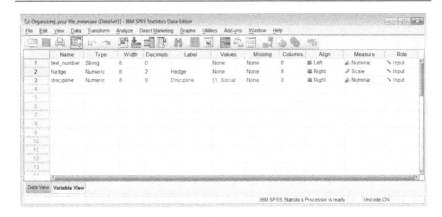

Figure 6.6 Adding variables in SPSS

a variable in any calculations; it is more like a reference for us to know which text file the data is coming from). So it will be string, and it will be a nominal type of data (all strings are nominal). (See Figure 6.6.)

Now that this is all set, let's turn to our "Data View" to see how the data will need to be entered. First, as we see in Figure 6.7, we have both variables and each in a column. In SPSS, all variables are in columns, and each observation is a different row. So, in our case, the dependent and independent variables are in the columns, and each text (each representing a presentation) will be in a different row.

Now we can start running some descriptive statistics.

Descriptive Statistics

In order to get information in a stratified manner for your levels, you want to give the following command. On the top bar with "File", "Edit", "View", choose the following set: Analyze → Descriptive Statistics → Explore to get to the window shown in Figure 6.8 (see p. 119).

Following our case study, as you see, your dependent variable (hedges) needs to be under "Dependent List" and your independent variable (discipline) needs to be under "Factor List". This way, your descriptive statistics will be calculated for each level (i.e., for each of your disciplines) versus giving just one mean score of the entire dataset you have. Run the statistics, and see to what extent the results by SPSS match the descriptive statistics we calculated earlier (they really should!). If you only want the numbers, click on "statistics"; if you want a boxplot (described in this chapter) and the numbers, click on "both". Explore what option you may have further by clicking on the "Options" button at the upper right-hand side.

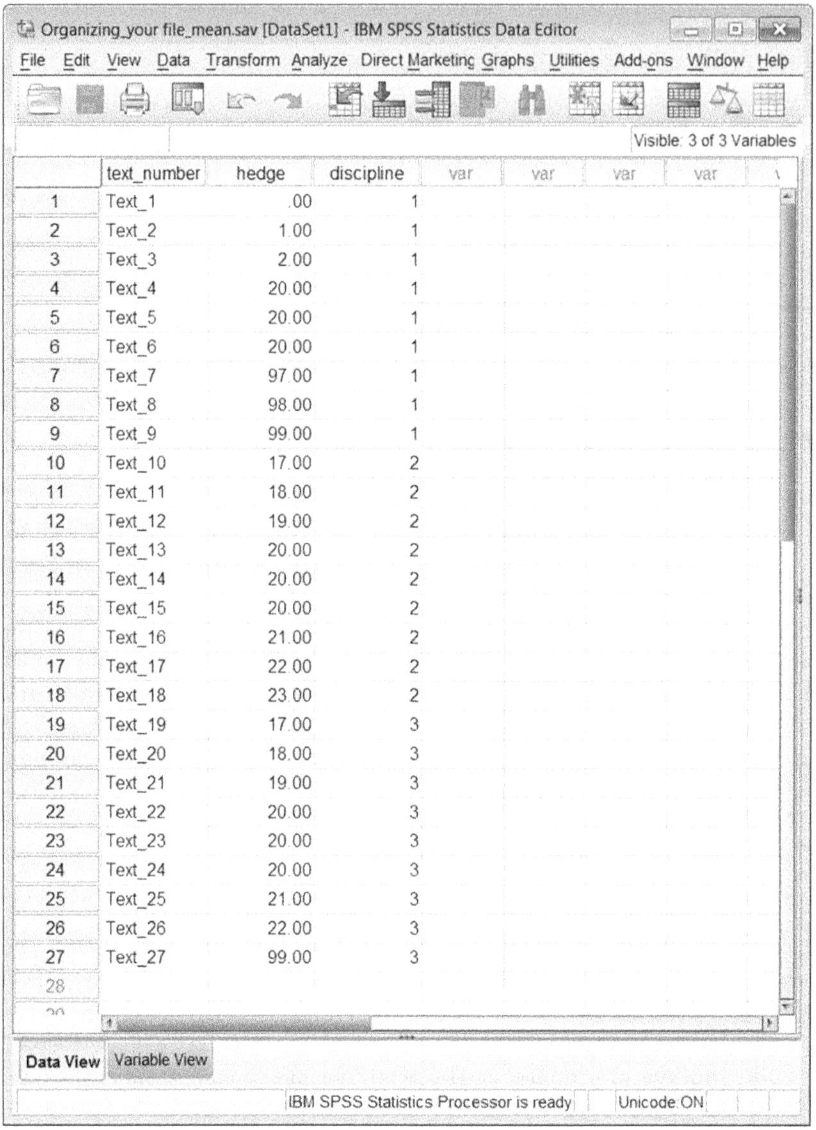

	text_number	hedge	discipline	var	var	var	var
1	Text_1	.00	1				
2	Text_2	1.00	1				
3	Text_3	2.00	1				
4	Text_4	20.00	1				
5	Text_5	20.00	1				
6	Text_6	20.00	1				
7	Text_7	97.00	1				
8	Text_8	98.00	1				
9	Text_9	99.00	1				
10	Text_10	17.00	2				
11	Text_11	18.00	2				
12	Text_12	19.00	2				
13	Text_13	20.00	2				
14	Text_14	20.00	2				
15	Text_15	20.00	2				
16	Text_16	21.00	2				
17	Text_17	22.00	2				
18	Text_18	23.00	2				
19	Text_19	17.00	3				
20	Text_20	18.00	3				
21	Text_21	19.00	3				
22	Text_22	20.00	3				
23	Text_23	20.00	3				
24	Text_24	20.00	3				
25	Text_25	21.00	3				
26	Text_26	22.00	3				
27	Text_27	99.00	3				
28							

Figure 6.7 Data view in SPSS

If you only wanted the numbers, it should look like the details in Table 6.3 listing all the necessary descriptive statistics for each of the disciplinary areas.

We believe the numbers generated by SPSS match the hand calculations we made in this chapter. In the next chapter, we will look at four different statistical tests that we can apply to our datasets. Before we do that, why don't you test your knowledge based on this chapter?

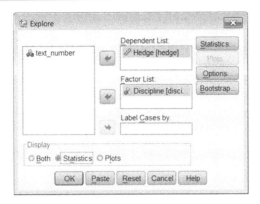

Figure 6.8 Descriptive statistics through "Explore" in SPSS

Table 6.3 Descriptive statistics for "hedges" in three disciplines through SPSS

Descriptives				
	Discipline		Statistic	Std. Error
Hedge	Social Sciences	Mean	39.66	14.84
		Median	20.00	
		Std. Deviation	44.52	
		Minimum	.00	
		Maximum	99.00	
		Range	99.00	
	Natural Sciences	Mean	20.00	.62
		Median	20.00	
		Std. Deviation	1.87	
		Minimum	17.00	
		Maximum	23.00	
		Range	6.00	
	Humanities	Mean	28.44	8.83
		Median	20.00	
		Std. Deviation	26.50	
		Minimum	17.00	
		Maximum	99.00	
		Range	82.00	

6.4 End of Chapter Exercises

6.4.1 Definitions

Briefly explain each of the following concepts/notions providing the mathematical formula where applicable, and give an example for each. Use your own words.

1. dependent and independent variables and their relationship to predictors and outcomes

2. population and sample and their relationship to each other
3. observations
4. standard deviation, variance (include calculation for each)
5. mean, median, mode
6. interval, nominal, ordinal scales
7. normed counts (importance and how to calculate it)
8. parametric versus non-parametric tests and inferential statistics

6.4.2 Variables

For each of the following research designs, determine what the dependent and the independent variables are, and whether they are interval, nominal, or ordinal scores. State the research question(s) and the null and alternative hypotheses.

1. Mary was curious to find out whether the instructor's gender or the course's level of instruction has a greater effect on informational focus in university classroom talk. She built a small but balanced corpus of randomly selected 30 class sessions from multiple corpora (MICASE, BASE, and others) where male and female instructors and levels of instruction (undergraduate, graduate) were both represented. She tagged the texts with a grammatical tagger, counted the appropriate part of speech tags (see Chapter 9 about tagging), and normed the feature counts to 1,000 words each. She defined informational focus by adding up the number of normed counts for nouns, attributive adjectives, nominalizations, and prepositions in each of the courses she included in her corpus.

2. Allen was interested in finding out what kinds of reduced forms correlate (if at all) in highly interactive university classes. He was particularly interested to see whether phrasal types of reduction (pronoun *it*, demonstrative pronouns, and indefinite pronouns) and clausal types of reduction (*that* deletion, contraction, *do* as a pro-verb) have any connection to one another. Examples of the different types of features are as follows:

pronoun *it*:	I read <u>it</u> and graded <u>it</u>.
demonstrative pronoun:	Look at <u>this</u> here.
indefinite pronouns:	Does <u>anyone</u> have an answer?
that deletion:	I believe [that] you are right.
contraction:	I'<u>ll</u> do that next week.
do as pro-verb:	I like pies and he <u>does</u> too.

Note

1 To calculate the normed counts, we typically take the frequency of the linguistic feature itself, divide it by the total number of words in the given text and

multiply it with a number (typically 1,000) for each observation. That is, let's say Text 1 has 45 first person pronouns, and it is 1,553 words long. Then we will calculate the normed count to 1,000 words (as if the text were that long) by (45 / 1,553) * 1,000 and we get 28.97. This way, we translated a nominal score into an interval score. Also, if texts have different lengths, this way we can actually compare the numbers. If Text 2 has 125 of the feature and the text is 3,552 words long, then the normed count will be (125 / 3,552) * 1,000, or exactly 35.19.

References

Csomay, E. (2002). Variation in academic lectures: Interactivity and level of instruction. In R. Reppen, S. Fitzmaurice, & D. Biber (Eds.), *Using corpora to explore linguistic variation* (pp. 203–224). John Benjamins.

Csomay, E. (2012). A corpus-based look at short turns in university classroom interaction. In E. Csomay (Ed.), *Contemporary perspectives on discourse and corpora*. Special issue of *Corpus Linguistics and Linguistic Theory*, 8(1), 103–128.

Hatch, E., & Lazaraton, A. (1991). *The research manual. Design and statistics for Applied Linguistics*. Heinle & Heinle.

Chapter 7

Statistical Tests (ANOVAs, Chi-Square, Pearson Correlation)

7.1 Difference Tests
7.2 Relationship Tests
7.3 How to Go About Getting the Statistical Results
7.4 Effect Size (Cohen's *d*)
7.5 End of Chapter Exercises

7.1 Difference Tests

When doing difference tests (e.g., One-Way ANOVA or Two-Way ANOVA), we test whether there is a statistically significant difference in the average scores, i.e., mean, between two or more variables. The goal of difference tests is to see the extent to which the independent variable(s) is/are responsible for the variability in the dependent variable. That is, we are interested in how one or more variables affect another variable. We can make claims about cause and effect, i.e., one variable changes because another variable has a profound (statistically significant) effect on it. We cannot talk about the results in terms of more or less significant, however. Once the results are statistically significant, we can investigate where the differences are with post-hoc tests and how strong the association between the dependent and independent variable is with *Cohen's d* measures, or more typically with R^2.

7.1.1 One-Way ANOVA (Analysis of Variance)

We can do a One-Way ANOVA test when we have one dependent variable and one independent variable, the latter with more than two levels (see example below). The dependent variable has to be an interval score, and the independent variable has to be nominal. With parametric tests, like One-Way ANOVA, we can generalize to the population that the sample was drawn from. Conceptually, with a One-Way ANOVA we are interested in

DOI: 10.4324/9781003363309-10

identifying the change in the dependent variable and associate the change with the manipulation of the independent variable. More specifically, we seek to find out whether the variability in the dependent variable is due to the variability of the scores within each level of the independent variable <u>or</u> across the levels (or groups) we are comparing. That is, One-Way ANOVA assesses whether the differences in mean scores are attributed to the variability within the groups or across the groups. If the ratio of these two measures is small – that is, if the "across-group" variation is small relative to the "within-group" variation – there is no statistical difference. If, however, the "across-group" variation is large relative to the "within-group" variation, there is a statistically significant difference across the groups. That is, the larger this ratio between the "within-group" variability measures and the "across-group" variability measures (F score), the more likely that the difference between the means across the groups is significant.

Assumptions and requirements with ANOVA:

1. We have one dependent and one independent variable, the latter with three or more levels.
2. The dependent variable must be reported in interval scores (e.g., normed counts for linguistic features) and must be continuous, and the independent variable must be nominal.
3. Measured variables must be independent (not repeated).
4. Normal distribution of scores is expected in each group.
5. Number of observations is equal in each group (a balanced design), although it is only necessary when we do calculations by hand. The statistical package (e.g., SPSS[1]) accounts for an imbalance.
6. Values/categories on independent and dependent variables must be mutually exclusive and exhaustive.
7. Cell values cannot be too small. A minimum of five observations per cell is necessary for each level of the independent variable.

EXAMPLE

As an example, let's say you are investigating university classrooms as your context. You analyze your context for all the situational variables outlined in Chapter 2, and you realize that discipline may be a situational variable in the academic context that may have an effect on how language is used in the classrooms. In fact, you have read earlier that the use of pronouns may vary depending on the discipline. Based on your readings, you also know that first person pronouns are more apparent in spoken discourse, and have been associated with situations where the discourse is produced under more involved production circumstances (e.g., where the participants share the same physical space, allowing for the potential of immediate involvement in interaction). Knowing all of this, you isolate this one pro-noun type because you are interested in the use of first person pronouns (*I, me, we, us*). More specifically, you would like to find out whether there is a significant difference in the use of first person pronouns in different disciplines (more than two).

You formulate your research question in one of two ways:

1. How does the use of first person pronouns differ across disciplines? Or
2. Is there a difference in first person pronoun use across disciplines?

The dependent variable is the composite normed score for the first per-son pronouns as listed above (instead of using frequency scores, which are nominal, use normed counts – an interval score), and the one independ-ent variable is discipline with three levels (nominal score with no numeric value). The three levels are the three disciplinary areas: Business, Humani-ties, and Natural Sciences.

You formulate your hypothesis:

H_0: There is no statistically significant difference in the use of first person pronouns across the three disciplines.
H_1: There is a statistically significant difference in the use of first person pronouns across the three disciplines.

The statistical test to use is One-Way ANOVA (one dependent variable [first person pronouns] with interval scores [normed to a thousand words] and one independent variable [discipline] with nominal scores and with multiple levels, in this case, three disciplines). The significance level is set at the .05 level, and to locate where the differences are in case the ANOVA results in a significant difference, we will use a Scheffe post-hoc test.

To illustrate how the statistical program calculates the F score, we will do a step-by-step demonstration. Table 7.1 below shows the fictive nor-med counts for the three disciplines. Once again, as we saw in Chapter 6

Table 7.1 First person pronoun data in SPSS data view format

Text number	First person pronoun normed count	Discipline
Text 1	3	1
Text 2	7	2
Text 3	8	3
Text 4	10	3
Text 5	12	3
Text 6	3	1
...		

(Section 6.3.1), these numbers are entered into SPSS, as illustrated in Table 7.1 below. Each observation (i.e., each text with each normed count) will be in a different row. The two variables are: First person pronoun use in each text normed to 1,000 words (interval variable) and Discipline (nominal with three levels: 1 = Business; 2 = Humanities; 3 = Natural Sciences).

But in this chapter, we will go through the steps of calculating the One-Way ANOVA by hand. For this reason, and for hand-counting the ANOVA, we will use a different type of organization, as it is easier to see what is happening within the groups when listed by group (Table 7.2).

In calculating the F score (the ratio for the mean sum of squares between and across groups), we need to take several steps. Conceptually, we are looking for the mean score for each group and then the variation as to how the scores are dispersed or spread (i.e., how far away each score is from the mean). This way, we can tell whether the variance can be attributed to variation inside each group or across the groups.

We take eight steps to do the calculations and determine where the differences lie. The following are the eight steps:

Step 1: Calculate the mean score for each group and for the entire dataset.
Step 2: Calculate distances across scores (and square them).
Step 3: Calculate degrees of freedom.
Step 4: Calculate mean sum of squares.
Step 5: Calculate F score.
Step 6: Determine whether the F score is significant.
Step 7: Calculate strength of association.
Step 8: Locate the differences with post-hoc tests.

Step 1: Calculate the mean score for each group and for the entire dataset.

Table 7.2 Calculating the mean score for each group

Business	Humanities	Natural Sciences
3	7	8
3	8	10
4	9	12
4	7	8
5	8	16
5	9	18

$\bar{X}_{Business} = 4$ $\bar{X}_{Humanities} = 8$ $\bar{X}_{Nat.sci.} = 12$ $\bar{X}_{Total} = 8$

Step 2: Calculate distances across scores.

Before we get into details in this area, it is necessary to make the difference between two notions: a) a score being x mean away from another score, and b) a score being x value away from the mean. The following is the explanation for the difference between these two notions:

a)   If a score is x mean away from another score, it means that we are measuring the distance in the value of the mean score. Let's assume, for example, that Mean = 4; Score(1) = 2; and Score(2) = 10. In this case, Score(2) is two means away from Score(1) because the difference between Score(1) and Score(2) is eight, and that is exactly two times the mean.

b)   If a score is x value away from the mean, it means that we simply calculate the difference between the mean and the given score and get a value as a result. Let's assume that Mean = 4; Score(1) = 2; and Score(2) = 10. In this case, the difference between Score(1) and the mean is –2 (2–4 = –2) and the difference between the mean and Score(2) is 6 "points/values" away from the mean. Hence, the former, Score(1), is –2 points or values away from the mean (on the negative side) while the latter, Score(2), is 6 points away from the mean (on the positive side).

In our calculations, we will mostly use the second type of distance measure. In looking at how the scores are dispersed, we need to calculate a) the distance between the individual score and its own group's mean, b) the distance between the group mean and the mean for the grand total, and c) the distance between the individual score and the mean for the grand total.

We will work with the following terminology: within sum of squares (SS_W) (the sum of squares within each group), between sum of squares (SS_B) (the sum of squares across groups), total sum of squares (SS_T) (the sum of squares for the entire dataset), degree of freedom within (Df_W) (degree of freedom within each group) and degree of freedom between (Df_B) (degree of freedom across groups).

a)   *Within each group: How far is each score from its own group's mean?*

To calculate the within-group sum of squares (SS_W or group variance), take each individual score (x) minus the mean for its group ($\overline{X}$ group), and square it. Add values gained this way for each group; then add each group together. You will get the within sum of squares (SS_W), or group variance (see Table 7.3).

Table 7.3 Calculating sum of squares within groups

Business			Humanities			Natural Sciences			Total
Raw score	$x - \bar{X}$ group	Squared value	Raw score	$x - \bar{X}$ group	Squared value	Raw score	$x - \bar{X}$ group	Squared value	
3	3–4 = –1	1	7	7–8 = –1	1	8	8–12 = –4	16	
3	3–4 = –1	1	8	8–8 = 0	0	10	10–12 = –2	4	
4	4–4 = 0	0	9	9–8 = 1	1	12	12–12 = 0	0	
4	4–4 = 0	0	7	7–8 = –1	1	8	8–12 = –4	16	
5	5–4 = 1	1	8	8–8 = 0	0	16	16–12 = 4	16	
5	5–4 = 1	1	9	9–8 = 1	1	18	18–12 = 6	36	
Total		4			4			88	96

$$SS_W = \sum \left(x - \bar{X} \text{ group}\right)^2$$

$$\bar{X}_{Business} = 4 \quad \bar{X}_{Humanities} = 8 \quad \bar{X}_{Nat.sci.} = 12$$

$$SS_W = 96$$

b) *Between groups: How far is each group from the total mean?*
   To calculate the between-group sum of squares (SS_B) (between-group variance), take each group mean ($\bar{X}$ group) minus the mean for the total ($\bar{X}$ total), square it and multiply by the number of observations in the given group (N_{group}). Do the same for each group and add up all results (see Table 7.4).

$$\bar{X}_{Total} = 8 \quad N_{group} = 6 \quad N_{Total} = 18 \ (6 \text{ in each group x 3 groups})$$

$$SS_B = \sum N \left(\bar{X} \text{ group} - \bar{X} \text{ total}\right)^2$$

Between sum of squares:

$$SS_B = 192$$

c) *Total sum of squares*
   To calculate the total sum of squares, take each score (x) minus the total mean ($\bar{X}$), square it and sum it up (see Table 7.5).

$$SS_T = \sum \left(x - \bar{X} \text{ total}\right)^2$$

$$SS_T = 288$$

An easier way to calculate this score is by adding up the "within" and "between" sum of square values calculated before: $SS_W + SS_B = SS_T$ (96 + 192 = 288).

Table 7.4 Calculating sum of squares between (across) groups

	Business	Humanities	Natural Sciences	Total
	6 x (4–8)²	6 x (8–8)²	6 x (12–8)²	
	6 x 16	6 x 0	6 x 16	
Total	96	0	96	192

Table 7.5 Calculating sum of squares total

Business			Humanities			Natural Sciences			Total
Raw score	$x - \bar{X}$ total	Squared value	Raw score	$x - \bar{X}$ total	Squared value	Raw score	$x - \bar{X}$ total	Squared value	
3	3–8 = –5	25	7	7–8 = –1	1	8	8–8 = 0	0	
3	3–8 = –5	25	8	8–8 = 0	0	10	10–8 = 2	4	
4	4–8 = –4	16	9	9–8 = 1	1	12	12–8 = 4	16	
4	4–8 = –4	16	7	7–8 = –1	1	8	8–8 = 0	0	
5	5–8 = –3	9	8	8–8 = 0	0	16	16–8 = 8	64	
5	5–8 = –3	9	9	9–8 = 1	1	18	18–8 = 10	100	
Total		100			4			184	288

Step 3: Calculate degrees of freedom.

Conceptually, the degree of freedom "refers to the quantities that can vary if others are given" (Hatch & Lazaraton, 1991:254). For example, if you know A and B in the following equation, there is no degree of freedom for the value to change for C: $A + B = C$; but if you do not know B, then there is one degree of freedom for you to change that will also change the results for C. The degree of freedom values apply to datasets as well as groups (see a YouTube tutorial on how to calculate the degree of freedom and why it is important here: www.youtube.com/watch?v=rATNoxKg1yA). Here, we have to calculate two types of degree of freedom.

Df_W (degree of freedom within groups) = all observations minus # of groups

$$Df_W = N - N_{group}$$

For our dataset: $18 - 3 = 15$, so our $Df_W = 15$.

Six observations in three disciplinary areas (6 x 3) minus three groups.

Df_B (degree of freedom between groups) = # of groups minus 1

$$Df_B = N_{group} - 1$$

For our dataset: $3 - 1 = 2$, so our $Df_B = 2$.

This will be important in looking up whether our F score is significant.

Step 4: Calculate mean sum of squares.

As an intermediary step between the distance calculations and the degree of freedom, we need an average of the squares. We will use the mean squares within-group (MS_W), and the mean squares between groups (MS_B) as a final step before being able to arrive at the F score. The mean square within the group is the within sum of squares divided by within degree of freedom.

For our dataset: $96/15 = 6.4$

The mean square is between sum of squares divided by degree of freedom between groups.

$$MS_B = \frac{SS_B}{Df_B}$$

For our dataset: $192/2 = 96$

Step 5: Calculate F score.
The F score equals MS_B divided by MS_W.

$$F = \frac{MS_B}{MS_W}$$

For our study: $F = 96/6.4 = 15$, so our $F = 15$.

Step 6: Determine whether the F score is significant.
We can determine whether the F score is significant by looking up the value in a chart in juxtaposition with the degrees of freedom. We looked up the critical value for significance for the two degrees of freedom. In such tables, on the side going down are the degree of freedom values for within groups and on the top going across the page are the degree of freedom values for across groups.

The critical value for .05 level is 3.68 or higher. Our F score ended up at a value of 15. Clearly, this is more than 3.68, and therefore, the F value represents statistical significance. In fact, if we look at the $p < .01$ level, it is significant there as well. The critical value for that is 6.36, and our F score of 15 is higher than that.

This means that the variation of scores across the groups is larger than the variation within the groups. That is, we can reject the null hypothesis, which states that "there is no statistically significant difference across the disciplines in the use of first person pronouns". Hence, we accept the alternative hypothesis, which states that "there is a statistically significant difference in the use of first person pronouns across disciplines". What we do not know yet, however, is how strong the association is between the two variables (dependent and independent) and where the differences lie. Below are Tables 7.6 and 7.7, respectively, showing how the statistical program SPSS reports on the descriptive statistics and on the One-Way ANOVA results.

Table 7.7 has all the numbers we have calculated in the process by hand previously. Check them out!

Step 7: Calculate the strength of association.
The strength of association tells us the "proportion of the variability in the dependent variable that can be accounted for by the independent variable" (Hatch & Lazaraton, 1991:330).

To calculate the R-squared for the One-Way ANOVA, we take the sum of squares between groups divided by the total sum of squares.

$$R^2 = \frac{SS_B}{SS_T}$$

Table 7.6 Descriptive statistics for first person pronoun

	N	Mean	Std. deviation	Minimum	Maximum
Business	6	4.00	.894	3	5
Humanities	6	8.00	.894	7	9
Natural Sciences	6	12.00	4.195	8	18
Total	18	8.00	4.116	3	18

Table 7.7 One-Way ANOVA results for first person pronouns

	Sum of squares	df	Mean square	F	Sig.
Between groups	192.00	2	96.00	15.00	.000
Within groups	96.00	15	6.40		
Total	288.00	17			

In our example,

$$R^2 = 192/288 = .666$$

$R^2 = .666$ means that 66% of the variance in the first person pronoun use can be accounted for by the discipline. That is, if you know the discipline, you can predict the use of pronouns more than half the time. Or, by knowing the first person pronoun score, we are able to predict which discipline it comes from with quite good certainty – more than half the time.

Step 8: Locate the differences with post-hoc tests.
With identifying the F score's significance, we can only say that there is a statistically significant difference in the use of, in our case, first person pronouns. What we cannot say is where the statistically significant differences are exactly. In order to be able to say that, we can use a range of post-hoc tests, including Scheffe, Tukey, Bonferroni, Duncan, or LSD. We are using Scheffe for the current question and dataset to illustrate how this works. Table 7.8 was, again, created by SPSS (Statistical Package for Social Sciences).

As Table 7.8 shows, the mean difference across each of the three disciplines is statistically significant. To determine where the significant differences actually lie and which direction they go, we need to look at each pair from Table 7.8 to say the following:

Table 7.8 Post-hoc test (Scheffe) results

(I) Discipline	(J) Discipline	Mean difference (I-J)	Std. error	Sig.	95% Confidence interval	
					Lower bound	Upper bound
Business	Humanities	−4.00(*)	1.461	.048	−7.96	−.04
	Natural Sciences	−8.00(*)	1.461	.000	−11.96	−4.04
Humanities	Business	4.00(*)	1.461	.048	.04	7.96
	Natural Sciences	−4.00(*)	1.461	.048	−7.96	−.04
Natural Sciences	Business	8.00(*)	1.461	.000	4.04	11.96
	Humanities	4.00(*)	1.461	.048	.04	7.96

* The mean difference is significant at the .05 level (as we also see in the Sig. column, all values are below p<.05)

1. Business – Humanities: The Business mean is 4 values lower than the Humanities mean (hence the negative number). Looking at our mean scores, it is true, since the Business mean was 4 and the Humanities mean was 8. Throughout the analysis, this was considered to be a statistically significant difference.
2. Business – Natural Sciences: The Business mean is 8 values lower than the Natural Sciences mean (hence the negative number). Looking at our mean scores, it is true, since the Business mean was 4 and the Natural Sciences mean was 12. Throughout the analysis, this was considered to be a statistically significant difference.
3. Humanities – Natural Sciences: The Humanities mean is 4 values lower than the Natural Sciences mean (hence the negative number). Looking at our mean scores, it is true, since the Humanities mean was 8 and the Natural Sciences mean was 12. Throughout the analysis, this was considered to be a statistically significant difference.

The rest of the information in the table is a repetition of this but with reversed direction. If we look at our original mean scores, it is true that the Business mean was 4, the Humanities mean was 8, and the Natural Sciences mean was 12. And now we know that these differences are, in fact, statistically significant.

INTERPRETATION

Based on previous readings, we know that first person pronouns are typically associated with a communicative context where language is produced in a shared physical space and under involved production circumstances, allowing for the potential of interaction. We also know through the situational analysis that disciplines may differ in the way the material is presented, and so we want to know to what extent first person pronouns would be an indicator of such difference. The statistical results in our mini-study showed that there is a statistically significant difference across disciplines, and that significantly more first person pronouns are used in Natural Sciences than in either one of the other two disciplines. In addition, it also shows that when compared to Humanities, Business also uses significantly fewer first person pronouns. These results indicate that in Natural Sciences classrooms, language features seem to be similar to those in spoken discourse (rather than written), which then is associated with discourse produced under involved production circumstances suggesting interaction. The fact that Business showed the least number of personal pronouns may be attributed to less interaction in the classroom, and more teacher talk perhaps.

7.1.2 Two-Way ANOVA

We do a Two-Way ANOVA test when we have one dependent variable, and at least two independent variables that could have two or more levels each. As with other parametric tests, the dependent variable has to be an interval score (as the mean has to be the best measure of central tendency and the standard deviation has to be the best measure of dispersion), and the independent variables have to be nominal. With parametric tests, like the Two-Way ANOVA, we can generalize to the population that the sample was drawn from. Conceptually, the Two-Way ANOVA helps us identify which one of the two (or both) independent variables is (are) responsible for the variability in the dependent variable. More specifically, the question is whether the variability in the dependent variable is due to one or both independent variables. Again, we are looking at the variability of the scores within each level group versus across the levels but not only for one independent variable as we did with the One-Way ANOVA but two. That is, the Two-Way ANOVA assesses whether the difference in mean scores is attributed to the variability within or across the level groups when it comes to two different variables and their combinations. Again, if the cross-group variation is large relative to the within-group variation, there is a statistically significant difference across the groups. That is, the larger this ratio between within-group variability measures and across-group variability measures (F score), the more likely that the difference between the means across the groups is significant. Although we would be using the same calculations if we wanted to calculate a Two-Way ANOVA by hand, as we have just done with the One-Way ANOVA, the computation becomes rather complex with two variables; hence, we will not do that by hand. We will, however, rely on the statistical package to give us the results (as we see it is pretty reliable!). What we need to be careful of here is the interpretation of the results.

EXAMPLE

As you have attended classes at the university, you noticed that teachers talk differently in classes not only from different disciplines (as we have seen the example before), but also in classes with different educational levels. Your primary investigation is discipline but it seems that level of instruction may also be a variable that could intervene in the variability of the data, and you are hoping that it does not affect your previous findings. All in all, you do not know whether the language change is attributed to only one of the variables (discipline/level) or the two together (discipline and level). In your situational analysis then, you take discipline as your main variable, and level of instruction as another, intervening variable. As for the teacher "talking differently", you continue to believe that, based on your previous readings, first person pronoun use is what makes the difference.

First, you formulate your research question in one of two ways:

1. How does the use of first person pronouns differ across disciplines and levels of instruction? OR
2. Is there a difference in first person pronoun use across disciplines or across levels of instruction?
3. Is there an interaction between discipline and level of instruction in terms of first person pronoun use?

The dependent variable is first person pronouns (use normed counts as discussed before, as it is an interval score), and the two independent variables are discipline (with three levels) and level of instruction (with three levels). The three levels for the independent variable "discipline" are Business, Education, and Natural Sciences, and the three levels for the independent variable "instruction" are lower-division undergraduate, upper-division undergraduate, and graduate.

Second, you formulate your hypothesis:

H_0: There is no effect on first person pronoun use for discipline or level instruction and there is no effect for the interaction.
H_1: There is an effect on first person pronoun use for discipline.
H_2: There is an effect on first person pronoun use for level of instruction.
H_3: There is an interaction effect on first person pronoun use.

The number of observations in each cell is summarized in Table 7.9.

The Two-Way ANOVA results provided by SPSS are in Table 7.10. As we see from Table 7.10, the significance value is lower than $p <.05$ (Sig.011) only for discipline. Hence, we can conclude with confidence that discipline alone is a significant factor in the varied use of first person pronouns. That is, level of instruction is not a significant factor alone, nor does it have an effect on the variation in the dependent variable (first person pronoun use). Since the interaction effect is also not significant (see line with Discipline * Level), the effect on the variation in the data was not moderated by the effect of level of instruction. It is clearly discipline alone that is responsible for the variation in the dataset.

Table 7.9 Distribution of cases in the dataset

	Value label	N
Discipline	Natural Sciences	10
	Education	10
	Business	10
Level	Lower division	13
	Upper division	6
	Graduate	11

Table 7.10 Two-Way ANOVA results for first person pronouns

Source	Type III sum of squares	df	Mean square	F	Sig.
Corrected model	2245.306[a]	8	280.663	2.706	.032
Intercept	31131.297	1	31131.297	300.136	.000
Discipline	**1154.974**	**2**	**577.487**	**5.568**	**.011**
Level	77.000	2	38.500	.371	.694
Discipline * level	893.091	4	223.273	2.153	.110
Error	2178.206	21	103.724		
Total	46476.120	30			
Corrected total	4423.512	29			

a. R Squared = .508 (Adjusted R Squared = .320)

INTERPRETATION

We set out to investigate whether discipline accounts for the variability in our data. At the same time, we also realized that in the academic context, an intervening variable, i.e., level of instruction, may have an effect on this variability as well. We tested this by running a Two-Way ANOVA to see what effect level of instruction may have. Based on the results above, we can conclude that discipline alone accounts for the variability in the data, and level has no effect on this variability. This means that there is a consistent change in the use of first person pronouns across disciplines, irrespective of whether the class is an undergraduate lower- or upper-division class, or a graduate class. Post-hoc tests could identify where exactly the differences are. It turns out that first person pronouns are used most frequently in Education classes, indicating a more interactive class than in the other two disciplines.

A word of warning: It must be noted that if the interaction effect is significant (that is, if $p <.05$ or lower in the line with the two variables juxtaposed Variable 1 * Variable 2), we cannot isolate any of the variables as significant even if they show a significant result on their own. Consider the following results (see Table 7.11) in terms of significance level and instead of what we had before (we are just doing this for the sake of the exercise – the numbers are not true results).

In this dataset, each of the independent variables is significantly marking the variation in the first person pronoun use. At the same time, the interaction measure (Discipline * Level) is also significant with a $p <.05$. This means that neither discipline nor level of instruction alone is responsible for the variability in the use of first person pronouns. Instead, the two variables together cause the change in the dataset. In other words, we cannot say that, for example, Natural Sciences consistently use more first -person pronouns than Humanities, because their use of pronouns is connected to the level of instruction. Apparently, they use more in their lower and graduate classes, but not in the upper-division undergraduate classes. This variation is also true for the other two disciplines, and so discipline alone is not a factor for the change in the dependent variable. It also depends on the level of education at least as robustly. All in all, the interaction effect, if significant, overrides the effect of the individual independent variables.

Table 7.11 Two-Way ANOVA results with significant interaction

Source	F	Sig.
Corrected model	2.706	.032
Intercept	300.136	.000
Discipline	5.568	.011
Level	5.371	.000
Discipline * level	5.153	.00
Error		
Total		
Corrected total		

7.2 Relationship Tests

When doing relationship tests (e.g., Chi-square and Pearson correlation), we test the relationship between two or more variables. That is, we test how well they go together. We are not interested in how one variable affects another one, as that is the goal of a test of difference seen in previous sections. Therefore, we also cannot make claims of cause and effect with relationship tests. We can only talk about the results in terms of a strong or weak relationship between two or across many variables.

7.2.1 Chi-Square

With Chi-square tests, both the dependent and the independent variables can be nominal data. The results of non-parametric tests, like Chi-square, cannot be generalized to the population the sample was drawn from but we can ask questions related to the given dataset. Namely,

- Is there a relationship between two variables *in the dataset*?
- How strong is the relationship *in the data*?
- What is the direction and shape of the relationship *in the data*?
- Is the relationship due to some intervening variable(s) *in the data*?

Conceptually, we typically want to know whether there is a relationship between two variables (and their levels). Chi-square compares the actual observed frequencies of some phenomenon with the frequencies we would expect if there were no relationship at all between the two variables in the sampled dataset. That is, Chi-square tests our actual results against the null hypothesis (i.e., no relationship) and assesses whether the actual results are different enough to overcome a certain probability that they are due to sampling error. The further apart the observed and expected values are, the more likely it is to be a significant Chi-square.

   Assumptions and requirements:

1. The sample must be randomly drawn from the population.
2. Data must be reported in raw frequencies (not in scales, e.g., as percentages would be).
3. When frequencies of a phenomenon are counted, the frequency of non-occurrence will also have to be counted.
4. Measured variables must be independent.
5. Values/categories on independent and dependent variables must be mutually exclusive and exhaustive.
6. Observed frequencies cannot be too small; the expected cell frequency has to be at least 5.

With Chi-square, we also have One-Way and Two-Way designs. The difference between the two is simply how many levels each variable has. A One-Way design (see Table 7.12 below) would have a dependent nominal variable with no levels, and an independent variable with potentially two or more levels. For example, if you wanted to compare the raw frequency scores of a particular type of relative clause across registers, you would use a One-Way design, as shown in Table 7.12.

All in all, a One-Way Chi-square design would have one variable with no levels (in the case of relative clauses, you would not go into details about the different types of relative clauses but you would just simply pull them under one variable) and one variable with two or more levels (registers). On the other hand, a Two-Way design would have a dependent nominal variable with two or more levels and an independent nominal variable with two or more levels. Table 7.13 shows a Two-Way Chi-square design: one variable with two or more levels (e.g., articles: *a*, *an*, *the*, zero article) and one variable with two or more levels (position: subject or object).

Table 7.12 One-Way Chi-square table

	News	Fiction	Spoken	Academic
Wh-relative	15	5	10	25

We rarely use One-Way designs in our studies, and therefore, we will focus on a Two-Way design.[2]

EXAMPLE

Imagine that you would like to find out about the relationship between article type (*a*, *an*, *the*, zero article) and their position (subject or object). Here are the steps you need to take:

Step 1: Formulate your research question: Is there a relationship between type of article use and clause position?
Step 2: State your null hypothesis: H_0 – There is no relationship between type of article use and clause position. State your alternative hypothesis: H_1 – There is a relationship between type of article use and clause position.
Step 3: Create a cross tab of frequencies of two nominal variables, article and position.

Each cell reports on how many observations produced that combination of independent and dependent values (see Table 7.13 below). For example,

54 definite articles were found in nominal clauses in subject position, etc. Although this dataset looks good, we need to be aware of the cell sizes. Here are some of the rules:

- For a 1x2 or 2x2 table, expected frequency values in each cell must be at least 5.
- For a 2x3 table, expected frequencies should be at least 2.
- For a 2x4 or 3x3 table, if all frequencies but one are at least 5 and if the one small cell is at least 1, Chi-square is still a good approximation.

If you are worried about the frequencies in the cells, you could collapse categories that make sense. In the example above, the two types of in-definite articles (*a/an*) can be collapsed since their use is dependent on the word following them (whether the following word starts with a vowel or a consonant) and will not affect the syntactic position they are in. Table 7.13 shows the crosstab of frequencies.

If the article distribution were the same in subject and object positions, we would get an equal number of them across article types. So the questions are: "How far is this off?" and "Can we say that they are really off, and whether there is a difference, or not?" That is the real question. In other words, if there were no relationship between the article type and the position, we would get an even distribution of the frequencies. Considering this, the question is: "Is there a relationship between the article type and clause position?" We calculate what we would expect if there were no relationship and compare that with the existing dataset.

Table 7.13 Two-Way Chi-square table

	the	A	an	0
Subject	54	27	8	19
Object	92	49	3	44

First, we calculate the row and column totals (Tables 7.14 and 7.15).

Second, we calculate the expected value for each cell by taking the row total and the column total, multiplying the two, and dividing it by the grand total. Below is the formula.

$$f_{expected} = \frac{Row_{total} \times Column_{total}}{N}$$

For example, to calculate the expected value for the first cell ("the" in subject position) take 108 (*Row total*) times 146 (*Column total*) divided by 296 (N) = 53.27. Do the same for each cell (Table 7.16).

Finally, we can calculate the Chi-square (χ^2): Deduct the expected value from the observed value, square it, and divide it by the expected value, and add it all up (Table 7.17).

Table 7.14 Revised Chi-square table

	the	a/an	0	Total
Subject	54	35	19	108
Object	92	52	44	188

Table 7.15 Chi-Square calculations (row and column totals)

Observed values	the	a/an	0	Row total
Subject	54	35	19	108
Object	92	52	44	188
Column total	146	87	63	296

Table 7.16 Calculating expected values

Expected values	the	a/an	0
Subject	53.27	31.74	22.99
Object	92.73	55.26	40.01

Table 7.17 Calculating Chi-square value

	the			a/an			0		
	O—E	squared	sq/E	O—E	squared	sq/E	O—E	squared	sq/E
Subject	0.73	0.53	0.01	3.26	10.63	0.34	-3.99	15.92	0.69
Object	-0.73	0.53	0.01	-3.26	10.63	0.19	3.99	15.92	0.40
Total			0.02			0.53			1.09

$$Chi\ square\left(\chi^2\right) = \sum \frac{\left(f_{observed} - f_{expected}\right)^2}{f_{expected}}$$

$$\chi^2 = 1.64$$

Degree of freedom:

(# of Rows – 1) times (# of Columns – 1)
In our study: (2–1) × (3–1)

Critical value on the p <.05 for 2 df is 5.991
Our Chi-square value is 1.62, which is below the critical value –
therefore, not significant.

What does this mean? It means that we cannot reject the null hypothesis stating that there is no relationship between the article type and position. In other words, any of the articles could pretty much randomly occur in any position, as there is no relationship between the position and the type of article used. While this example may not have direct relevance to register studies, we could follow up with a register study. Instead of looking at the potential relationship between article type and syntactic position, the focus of the investigation would be to see whether one type of article, when in a certain position, occurs more often in one register over another, and versus in another position.

7.2.2 Correlation

Among the three different types of correlations (Pearson, Spearman Rank Order, and Point-Biserial), Pearson correlation is the most frequently used statistical procedure in corpus studies. With Pearson, we need interval data for both the dependent and independent variables.

Conceptually, we are looking for relationships between two or more variables in the dataset. Again, as with Chi-square, we do not look at how one variable affects the other but how they relate to each other. Therefore, the research question also aims at looking for relationships (whether strong or weak), and not differences (whether there is an effect or not).

The null hypothesis for difference studies (e.g., One-Way ANOVA) is like this: "There is no difference between the two variables with respect to some measure".

The null hypothesis for relationship studies is like this: "There is no relationship between two measures".

You noticed that *I mean* and *ok* often come as a package in spoken discourse. You also noticed that both teachers and students use it, but what you don't know is whether it's the same when they are presenting in front of an audience. Let's assume you would like to find out whether there is a relationship between the use of "I mean" and "ok". You have a small corpus of presentations comprising two sub-corpora: teacher presentations and student presentations. Let's say, the mean score for *I mean* used for teachers is 39.1, and for students, it is 42.5.

There is too much overlap between the two types of presentations in terms of "I mean" use. That is, if we did a difference type of test (e.g., like ANOVA), there would not be a significant difference between teacher and student presentations in terms of the use of "I mean". In other words, we would not be able to predict whose presentation it is by knowing the "I mean" count.

In contrast, the mean score for *ok* use for teachers is 150, and for students, it is 328. There is no overlap between the two types of presentations in terms of the use of "ok". That is, in a difference type of test (e.g., One-Way ANOVA), this would show a significant difference between teacher and student presentations in terms of "ok" use. That is, we could predict who gives the presentation by knowing the "ok" count.

"I Mean" and "Ok" Use in Two Settings: Teacher Presentation and Student Presentation

If the uses of the two expressions consistently overlapped, seeing a correlation may be nice. That is, if we knew that the count for one feature is high, we could know that the other feature count will also be high. So, the relationship between the two features would be strong.

With two interval variables, you want to see what the strength is between the two variables so you can predict the occurrence of one by knowing the occurrence of the other. If there is no correlation, there is no relationship. If there is a correlation, then that means that there is a relationship between the two variables. The questions to ask then are: a) what kind of relationship it is, and b) how strong the relationship is. There are two kinds of relationships: positive and negative. In positive relationships, if one score is high, the other score is also high. Translated to our question, if the "I mean" score is high, then the "ok" score will also be high. In a negative relationship, if one score is high, the other score is low. In our case, if the "I mean" score is high, the "ok" score would be consistently low.

The correlation coefficient (r) is between 0 and 1 (whether positive or negative depending on the direction of the correlation explained above), where zero means no correlation (i.e., absolutely no relationship), and +1 means perfect correlation with a 100% overlap.

+1............. 0...........−1

In terms of strength, we need to see at what percentage can we predict one over the other. The direct measure of strength is r^2, and we are looking at the percent overlap between 0 and 100%.

Let's have a visual about a potential dataset. Look at Figure 7.1. The data-point in light gray tells us that this text has 20 "ok" and 30 "I mean"

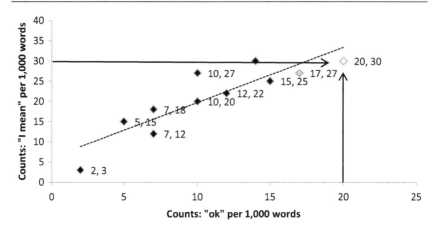

Figure 7.1 Correlation between "ok" and "I mean"

scores. The data-point in darker gray tells us that this text has 17 "ok" and 27 "I mean". There seems to be a consistent relationship between the use of "I mean" and "ok" in this dataset (as the straight dotted line indicates the pattern); that is, if one occurs, the other one also occurs, and it seems to be a positive relationship. The positive relationship means that if one occurs, the other one occurs too. The question is how consistent and how strong the relationship is between these two features in the entire dataset.

We can calculate the Person product *r* through Excel or SPSS. Table 7.18 was produced by SPSS, where *r* =.885, and that the correlation is statistically significant at the *p* <.01 level. While the significance does not matter that much in correlation studies (see below for more discussion on that), the bigger the *r* value (i.e., the closer it is to 1), the stronger the relationship is between the two variables. So, the magnitude tells us how well the two variables go together. As it is a positive value here, we can be certain that our dataset shows that the higher the number of the "ok" counts, the higher the number of the "I mean" counts.

Table 7.18 Correlations calculated by SPSS

		ok	I mean
Ok	Pearson correlation	1	.885**
	Sig. (2-tailed)		.000
	N	11	11
I mean	Pearson correlation	.885**	1
	Sig. (2-tailed)	.000	
	N	11	11

** Correlation is significant at the 0.01 level (2-tailed).

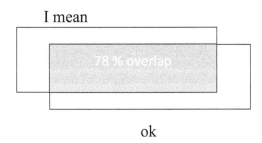

I mean

78 % overlap

ok

Figure 7.2 Overlap between "I mean" and "ok"

Next we calculate the r^2, which is the direct measure of strength between the two variables (or variance overlap, which is the variability of the data around the mean, if you recall). In our example, $r^2 =.783$ means that about 78% of the data has shared variation. Visually, it looks like Figure 7.2.

This means that 78% of the time we can predict that if one feature occurs, the other one occurs too. That is, "the magnitude of r^2 indicates the amount of variance in" one variable "which is accounted for by the other variable" or the other way around (Hatch & Lazaraton, 1991: 441). To translate this to our study here, it sounds like this: The amount of variance in the use of "I mean" is accounted for by the use of "ok".

What is a strong overlap and what is a weak one is hard to tell without knowing the question. If you wish to show that one text is very similar to another, the higher the overlap the better. What the cut-off point is (i.e., what counts as an acceptably strong correlation) depends on the field of study. In social science research in general, if the overlap is over 25%, it is considered very high. However, since it is genuine continuous data, there is no need for a cut-off point. The degree will depend on how the disciplines regard this as strong or not, and that is why no significance level is necessary.

Some useful hints when doing correlation studies:

1. Forget the groups. Whether there is a relationship between the two variables is the question.
2. Only use words like *strong* and *weak* and not significant when talking about correlations.
3. Be aware that there is a relationship between sample and correlation. Every correlation has a significance part in terms of correlating or not (as we have seen) and a strength part. The closer we get to a 100% relationship, the stronger the correlation is, but that increasing strength does not affect the significance of the correlation.

In this section, we only looked at how two linguistic variables may relate to one another (or what relationship they may have) but we can look at more than two at once. It is almost like going to a party where you try to figure out who is hanging out with whom and what characteristics they have. In any case, if you look at correlations of more linguistic variables at once, you can start characterizing texts for their comprehensive linguistic make-up. We will briefly discuss this and point you in that direction in the last chapter of this book.

INTERPRETATION

The interpretation here is simple: when one language feature occurs, the other one does as well. That is, there is a positive relationship between the two variables and so we can predict that if there is a high number of one, there will be a high number of the other as well. This kind of study becomes more interesting when we look at more than just two linguistic features co-occurring with one another; i.e., when we are able to detect how a number of features, when thrown in the same pot and having an effect on one another, will behave. This will be discussed in Chapter 9 further as we are looking ahead.

7.3 How to Go About Getting the Statistical Results

As in the previous chapter, we will show you how to get the results in SPSS for the four different tests you set out to investigate.

7.3.1 Difference Tests

One-Way ANOVA

To run a One-Way ANOVA test in SPSS, from the tabs select Analyze → Compare Means → One-Way ANOVA. Again, your "Dependent List" will contain the dependent variable. Although you could only have one dependent variable to test a One-Way ANOVA, if you want to run the test on more than one dependent variable at the same time (e.g., you want to see variation in hedges and also in noun use), instead of opening the window for each individually, you can list all of them under the dependent list. The program will take them one by one, and run the test on each separately. Your independent variable with multiple levels will go into the "Factor" window.

Two-Way ANOVA

To run a Two-Way ANOVA test in SPSS, from the tabs select Analyze → General Linear Model → Univariate. Again, you will put your dependent variable in the "Dependent Variable" field, and the independent variable will come under "Fixed Factor(s)" and your intervening variable (your second independent variable) will come under "Random factor(s)". You can also determine what "Post-hoc" test you may want to use in case only one variable significantly accounts for the variability of the data.

7.3.2 Relationship Tests

Chi-Square

To obtain Chi-square results, go to Analyze → Non-parametric tests → Legacy Dialogs → Chi-square. Again, your variables will go into the appropriate boxes and you can hit "run".

Pearson Correlation

To obtain Pearson correlation results, go to Analyze → Correlate → Bivariate Correlations, click on "Pearson". Again, your variables will go into the appropriate boxes, and you need to decide whether you want a one-tailed or a two-tailed analysis (see Chapter 6). Again, hit "run".

7.4 Effect Size

With each parametric or non-parametric statistical test, a strength of association (effect size) measure is calculated. This could be *Eta*-square, *R*-square, Cohen's *d*, and others. Conceptually, effect size measures point to how strong an association there is between the dependent and the independent variable. The larger the effect size, the stronger the relationship; that is, the more important the connection is between the two variables. In this section, we will focus on Cohen's *d* only as an effect size measure as this measure has been used more prominently in recent years.

7.4.1 Cohen's d

After determining statistical significance with parametric or non-parametric tests that compare two groups at a time, for example, with an Independent sample T-test (unlike ANOVA, which compares three or more groups), Cohen's *d* is used more and more frequently in applied linguistic research (Crawford et al., 2018; Wei & Hu, 2019; Wei et al., 2019) to measure effect size.

Cohen's *d* "expresses the mean difference between (or within) groups" (Plonsky, 2015: 31). Effect size measures "provide an estimate of the actual strength of the relationship or of the magnitude of the effect in question" (ibid.), allowing the researcher to use qualitative measures to describe the degree of difference between two groups. Cohen's d can be calculated easily in an Excel sheet by deducting the mean of one group from the mean of the other group and dividing the difference by the two groups' pooled standard deviation; that is,

$$\text{Cohen's } d = \frac{\bar{x}_1 - \bar{x}_2}{\sqrt{\dfrac{sd_1^2 + sd_2^2}{2}}}$$

Cohen's d effect sizes can take up positive or negative values depending on whether the larger or the smaller mean score enters the equation first. While there is no exact cut-off point for Cohen's d, researchers in applied linguistics typically consider ±0.40 a small effect size, ±0.70 a medium effect size, and ±1.00 and above a large effect size (Biber & Egbert, 2018; Crawford et al., 2018; Plonsky, 2015; Plonsky & Oswald, 2014).

EXAMPLE

Let's say, you want to see how important the difference is between students in one class over another in the use of academic vocabulary (adopted from Csomay, 2020). Your dependent variable is the percentage score of academic vocabulary use in student-written texts (continuous, interval score). Your independent variable (nominal) is the two groups (Group 1 and Group 2). You have 30 observations (i.e., 30 students whose texts you investigate) for each group. You may want to run an Independent T-test on your data just to see whether there is a statistically significant difference in the test scores between the two groups. The T-test will only be able to tell you this very fact (i.e., whether there is or there isn't a statistically significant difference between the two groups) but it will not be able to tell you how important those differences are. Cohen's d will allow you to think further about how important that difference may be. The larger the effect size measure, the more robust the differences are.

To calculate Cohen's d in Excel, the following steps need to be taken:

Step 1: Enter your data into Excel by creating two columns, one for each of the levels in your independent variable. (In the example above, one would be the use of academic vocabulary [in percentages] for one group and for the other group.)

Step 2: Calculate the means and standard deviations for each group.

Step 3: Calculate the Cohen's d score based on the measures in Step 2. The formula in Excel is: =(mean_gr_1-mean_gr_2)/SQRT((POWER(sd_gr_1,2)+POWER(sd_gr_2,2))/2) where mean_gr_1 is mean of Group

1, mean_gr_2 is mean of Group 2, SQRT is square root, POWER and 2 is for the second power, i.e., squared, sd_gr_1 is standard deviation for Group 1, and finally, sd_gr_2 is standard deviation for Group 2.

Step 4: Interpret the result.

INTERPRETATION

Let's say your results for Cohen's d were the following: $Mean_{group1}$ = 5.64, SD_{group1} = 1.58, and $Mean_{group2}$ = 9.22, SD_{group2} = 1.95. Your Cohen's d = –2.02 (adopted from Csomay, 2020). According to Plonsky (2015), your score of –2.02 for Cohen's d is a large effect size. It is a negative number because the mean score for Group 1 was smaller than the mean score for Group 2 and we deducted them from each other in this order. Had we deducted them in the reverse order, we would get the same value but a positive number. That means that the difference between the two groups in terms of their use of academic vocabulary use is, indeed, large, and there-fore, needs to be considered as an important one!

7.5 End of Chapter Exercises

After reviewing your answers to the scenarios in Section 6.4.2 in the previous chapter, determine what statistical test you would use selecting from the possible tests described in this chapter. With the data provided below, review Section 6.3, enter it into SPSS, and run the appropriate statistical test.

1.   Data for Question #1 in Section 6.4.2

Table 7.19 Normed counts for "Informational focus" in each class session recorded (text)

	Undergraduate	Graduate
Male	Text 1. 152.4	Text 1. 80.2
	Text 2. 156.8	Text 2. 80.9
	Text 3. 151.6	Text 3. 82.2
	Text 4. 160.5	Text 4. 81.4
	Text 5. 157.2	Text 5. 81.2
Female	Text 1. 155.4	Text 1. 100.2
	Text 2. 154.8	Text 2. 110.9
	Text 3. 155.6	Text 3. 115.2
	Text 4. 159.5	Text 4. 98.4
	Text 5. 156.2	Text 5. 91.2

2.   Results for Question #2 in Section 6.4.2

Looking at the output from SPSS in the table below what relationships can you see in the results?

Correlations

		That deletion	Contraction	DO as pro-verb	Pronoun IT	Demonstrative pronoun	Indefinite pronoun
That deletion	Pearson Correlation	1	.330	.076	.431*	.246	.133
	Sig. (2-tailed)		.075	.691	.017	.190	.485
	N	30	30	30	30	30	30
Contraction	Pearson Correlation	.330	1	.503**	.388*	.211	.219
	Sig. (2-tailed)	.075		.005	.034	.263	.244
	N	30	30	30	30	30	30
DO as pro-verb	Pearson Correlation	.076	.503**	1	.293	.419*	.375*
	Sig. (2-tailed)	.691	.005		.117	.021	.041
	N	30	30	30	30	30	30
Pronoun IT	Pearson Correlation	.431*	.388*	.293	1	.283	.088
	Sig. (2-tailed)	.017	.034	.117		.130	.646
	N	30	30	30	30	30	30
Demonstrative pronoun	Pearson Correlation	.246	.211	.419*	.283	1	.422*
	Sig. (2-tailed)	.190	.263	.021	.130		.020
	N	30	30	30	30	30	30
Indefinite pronoun	Pearson Correlation	.133	.219	.375*	.088	.422*	1
	Sig. (2-tailed)	.485	.244	.041	.646	.020	
	N	30	30	30	30	30	30

* Correlation is significant at the 0.05 level (2-tailed).
** Correlation is significant at the 0.01 level (2-tailed).

Figure 7.3 Correlation table for reduced forms

Notes

1 Statistical Package for the Social Sciences.
2 We must be careful as to how we select them in the corpus, though – and the best way to do so is to get a set of randomly selected relative clause sentences and continue our classification based on that.

References

Biber, D., & Egbert, J. (2018). *Register variation online.* Oxford University Press.
Crawford, W., McDonough, K., & Brun-Mercer, N. (2018). Identifying linguistic markers of collaboration in second language peer interaction: A lexico-grammatical approach. *TESOL Quarterly, 53*(1), 180–207.
Csomay, E. (2020). A corpus-based study of academic word use in EFL student writing. In U. Roemer, V. Cortes, & E. Friginal (Eds.), *Advances in corpus-based research on academic writing* (pp. 9–32). Benjamins.
Hatch, E., & Lazaraton, A. (1991). *The research manual. Design and statistics for Applied Linguistics.* Heinle & Heinle.

Plonsky, L. (2015). Statistical power, *p* values, descriptive statistics, and effect sizes: A "back-to-basics" approach to advancing quantitative methods in L2 research. In L. Plonsky (Ed.), *Advancing quantitative methods in second language research* (pp. 23–45). Routledge.

Plonsky, L., & Oswald, F. (2014). How big is "big"? Interpreting effect sizes in L2 research. *Language Learning, 64,* 878–912.

Wei, R., & Hu, Y. (2019). Exploring the relationship between multilingualism and tolerance of ambiguity: A survey study from an EFL context. *Bilingualism: Language and Cognition, 22*(5), 1209–1219.

Wei, R., Hu, Y., & Xiong, J. (2019). Effect size reporting practices in applied linguistics research: A study of one major journal. *Sage Open, 9*(2), 1–11.

Chapter 8

Doing Corpus Linguistics

8.1 Doing a Register (Functional) Analysis of Your Project
8.2 Situational Analysis
8.3 Linguistic Analysis
8.4 Functional Interpretation
8.5 Reporting on Your Project

The previous chapters of this book have discussed 1) how to do a register analysis (Chapter 2); 2) the types of software that you can use in corpus analysis (Chapter 3); 3) how to do corpus projects using existing corpora (Chapter 4); 4) how to build and structure your corpus for analysis (Chapter 5); and, 5) how to apply and interpret basic statistical techniques (Chapters 6–7). This chapter will guide you through the steps and procedures to actually put the corpus to use and to report on your research findings. In the following section, we will provide some guiding principles for how to go about answering your research question(s) using a register analysis framework and corpus methods. Then, we will describe the different parts of a research study and provide some guidelines for writing up and presenting your research project as well as suggest some approaches to how your corpus project can be assessed.

8.1 Doing a Register (Functional) Analysis of Your Project

As illustrated in Chapter 2, a register functional approach includes three components: 1) describing situational characteristics of texts; 2) identifying frequent linguistic characteristics of these texts; and 3) providing a functional interpretation of why these frequent linguistic features are found in the texts. In the following sections, we will discuss the steps in more detail. In order to illustrate some of the concepts in doing a situational and linguistic analysis along with a functional interpretation, we will refer

DOI: 10.4324/9781003363309-11

Table 8.1 A corpus of problem-solution essays written by Thai speakers of English

	Individual	Collaborative
# of texts	102	51
# of words	14,124	9,284
# of words/text	138.47	182.03

to a small corpus of English as Second-Language writers who were asked to produce problem–solution paragraphs in two different conditions. The research question for this study is: "Do collaborative and individual texts differ in terms of their use of lexico-grammatical features?" The texts from this corpus were collected under two different conditions: First, the students were placed into pairs and asked to write a problem-solution paragraph collaboratively. Later in the semester, each student had to write a problem-solution paragraph as part of an in-class examination. The essays were then typed and saved as text files with headers and codes to show the authors and topics of the essays. The corpus was also divided into two sub-corpora: one consisting of collaboratively written essays ($N = 51$) and another consisting of individual essays ($N = 102$). A description of the corpus is shown in Table 8.1.

This table provides the number of individual and collaborative essays, the total number of words in each sub-corpus, and the average number of words for the individual and collaborative texts. We will return to this table when we discuss the analysis of linguistic features in Section 8.3. However, before looking at how to search for linguistic features, we will first describe the method for completing a situational analysis.

8.2 Situational Analysis

As you recall in our discussion of register analysis in Chapter 2, the first step in a register functional analysis requires a description of the situational characteristics of your corpus. We follow the work of Biber (1988) and Biber and Conrad (2019) in our description of the situational characteristics. As discussed in Chapter 2, there are seven main components used to describe the context of a language text or "event". These are described in Table 8.2 below. The situational variables include information on the roles and relationships of the participants; the type of language used (whether it is written or spoken; whether it is edited or unplanned); the setting; the purpose of the communication; and the topic. In a sense, register analysis predicts that variation in (at least some of) these situational characteristics will result in variation in language use. In the table below, we provide some questions that are intended to guide you in your situational analysis.

Table 8.2 Situational characteristics of registers

Situational variables	Questions to consider when identifying situational variables
Participants	Addressor(s): Are the texts produced by a single writer or speaker or are there multiple writers/speakers in a single text?
	Addressee(s): Who is the intended audience? A single person, multiple people?
Relations among participants	Is there linguistic interaction between participants?
	Are there power or status differences among the participants?
	What is the nature of the personal relationships among participants (e.g., friends, co-workers, strangers)?
	Do the participants share different types of information or knowledge (e.g., personal information, topic-specific information)?
Channel	Is the language written or spoken? Is the language permanent (recorded or written) or is the language temporary (face-to-face conversation, television, telephone)?
Production circumstances	Is the language revised and edited, planned or unplanned?
Setting	Do the participants share the same place and time?
	Is the language used in a private or public setting?
	Does the language take place in the present or in the past (including the historical past)?
Communicative purposes	What is the general purpose of the language (e.g., to report, describe, tell a story, inform, explain, persuade, entertain)?
	What is the specific purpose of the language (e.g., describe methods, summarize sources, teach)?
	Is the language factual, hypothetical, imaginative, or opinion?
Topic	What is the general and specific topic of the language used?

Depending on the structure of your corpus as well as your research goal, projects that include sub-corpora should provide separate situational analyses for each sub-corpus. That way, any variation in language use can serve as a potential reason for variation across the two groups of texts. Should your project necessitate this, you can make a single table with multiple columns to illustrate the shared characteristics of the corpora as well as the characteristics that are different. A sample situational analysis of the problem-solution corpus is shown in Table 8.3 below. As we can see from this table, the texts differ in the relations among participants, the production circumstances, and topic. As discussed in Chapter 5, your corpus has already been built with a research question or set of research questions in

Table 8.3 Situational analysis of problem-solution essay corpus

	Sub-corpus A	Sub-corpus B
Participants	Second language writers of English Native language is Thai Intermediate level of English proficiency	Second language writers of English Native language is Thai Intermediate level of English proficiency
Relations among participants	**One writer**; teacher as audience	**Two writers of a single essay**; teacher as audience
Channel	Written	Written
Production circumstances	**Timed exam**	**Timed in-class activity**
Setting	Classroom	Classroom
Communicative purposes	Describe problem and propose a solution	Describe problem and propose a solution
Topic	**Lack of English in Thai teachers; World hunger; Protecting natural resources in parks**	**Shortage of teachers in Thailand; Videogame addiction among students**

mind; however, the situational analysis can be very helpful in describing and motivating your research question(s). For example, you could motivate your study by discussing the importance/relevance of any single or combination of these three situational variables with respect to second-language writing. When discussing results, the potential role of these three variables may also be relevant. For example, if the lexical and grammatical differences between the essays seemed more related to the topic than the relations among participants or the production circumstances, this would be an interesting finding that could be presented and discussed.

8.3 Linguistic Analysis

Once the situational analysis is completed, various tools can be used to search the corpus for relevant linguistic features. Although there are many different tools and methods (with new tools becoming available), two basic approaches can be used. As we mentioned in earlier chapters, the first involves searching for language patterns in your corpus without having any preconceived idea of what you might find. This type of method is sometimes referred to as "corpus-driven" because it utilizes tools to search the corpus for language features that you may not necessarily be aware of. Two useful tools in this approach are word lists and n-grams. To generate a word list, all of the individual texts can be loaded into AntConc (see Chapter 5 for details) and the word list function is used to provide a list of the most frequent words in the corpus. This same procedure can also be used with the collaborative texts to see if there are specific words that are frequent in one sub-corpus that may not be as frequent in another sub-corpus. Figure 8.1 provides a screenshot of the word list for the individual texts in the example corpus (also referred to as uni-grams in Chapter 3). We will look more closely at the word list findings below.

The "Clusters/N-Grams" function is another tool in AntConc that is useful when employing a corpus-driven method (see Section 3.3 for discussion of n-grams/lexical bundles). The size of n-grams can range from uni-grams (as discussed in Chapter 3 and illustrated in the word list function above) to longer sequences. Figure 8.2 shows the most frequent four-word n-grams in the individual problem-solution texts. These n-grams are found by using the "Clusters/N-gram" tab and then specifying the n-gram size (4)

Figure 8.1 Word list in a corpus of problem-solution essays written by Thai speakers of English

as well as the minimum frequency (5), using the tools found at the bottom of the screen (as shown in Figure 8.2). Note that you can change the size of the n-grams to look at bi-grams, tri-grams, and even longer sequences of words if you choose to do so. Note as well that next to the minimum frequency option in Figure 8.2, there is also an option for "Minimum range". This option allows you to select the minimum number of texts that contain at least one example of the n-gram. If this number is set to 1 (as seen in Figure 8.2), then this means it is possible that a frequent n-gram is not frequent in most of the texts but could just be frequent in one or more texts. Choosing a higher minimum frequency number will ensure that a feature is dispersed across a greater number of texts in the corpus. dispersion can also be understood by using the concordance plot function as discussed below.

Figure 8.2 4-grams in a corpus of problem-solution essays written by Thai speakers of English

The second general method to use is the "corpus-based method". If you choose to take a "corpus-based" approach, you already have an idea of the linguistic features that will be the focus of your research. This approach is used when previous corpus information guides the linguistic features used in the analysis. For example, previous corpus research has illustrated that face-to-face conversation has many first and second person pronouns. The high number of these pronouns can be understood by reference to the inter-actional nature of face-to-face conversation where speakers often make reference to themselves as well as to the other participants of the conversation. This corpus-informed fact can serve as a reason to look for the frequency of first and second person pronouns in corpora that do not involve face-to-face conversation but that also include examples of spoken language in other contexts (such as academic lectures, where the purpose of communication is primarily informational). If one were to find a high number of first and second person pronouns in academic lectures, this may be indicative of the interactional nature of academic lectures. In this sense, corpus-informed searches can be attributed to the fact that certain linguistic features have specific functions associated with them (as illustrated in previous research) so that the occurrence in another corpus with different situational characteristics can be related to this same functional interpretation.

In one sense, the distinction between corpus-driven and corpus-based research methods can be misleading. At least with respect to a register functional approach, any feature that is identified through a corpus-driven approach will still merit closer scrutiny and analysis in the corpus. If, for example, a word list shows that one particular word is more frequent in one sub-corpus than in another (a corpus-driven method), then the researcher will still need to look at the distribution and use of this feature more closely in the corpus by investigating its use in some more detail. One might argue that this second step can be seen as corpus-based because it identifies features in the corpus that merit further attention. On the other hand, it might also be argued that the feature was not identified by previous corpus-based research so it is, by definition, not corpus-based. We see the merits of both approaches in trying to understand language use and would encourage the use of both methods, especially in the smaller corpora that serve as the basis for your projects.

In Chapter 5, we mentioned the importance of building sub-corpora of fairly equal sizes (see Section 5.3). Sometimes this is not possible, as in the case of the problem-solution corpus described above. Since the design of this study was focused on writing paragraphs, the researchers had no control over the length of the texts. Furthermore, because the same writers produced texts both individually and collaboratively, it was not possible to simply add more collaborative texts to make the corpora equal. If your project involves comparing the frequency findings of sub-corpora in your corpus (or to another existing corpus), you will need to employ a simple statistical procedure known as "normalization" to ensure that your results are comparable (see a brief mention of this in Chapter 6). Normalization allows frequency counts taken from corpora of different sizes to be compared by providing a count of the frequency of the feature in a similar number of words.

Table 8.4 provides the five most frequent words in both the individual and collaborative essays. The most frequent word in the individual corpus is "the" and occurs 726 times; in the collaborative corpus, "the" occurs 425 times. The most frequent word in the collaborative corpus is "to" and occurs 432 times; in the individual corpus, "to" occurs 524 times. Although the frequency of both "the" and "to" is higher in the individual texts, the sub-corpora are not of equal size (see Table 8.1). If we want to compare the frequency in two corpora that do not contain equal words, we can normalize the counts and then use the normalized (or normed) counts as the basis for comparison. To do this, we divide the frequency of a given feature by the total number of words in the corpus and then multiply this by a reference number that will tell us how frequently this word (or feature) occurs per x number of words. In this case, we will use 1,000 as the reference number. The results would show that individual "the" occurs 51.40 times per 1,000 words ($726 / 14{,}124 \times 1{,}000 = 51.40$) and collaborative "the" occurs 45.77 times per 1,000 words ($425 / 9{,}284 \times 100 = 45.77$). When considering the frequency comparison of the word "the" in the two sub-corpora, we can then compare 51.40 (individual) with 45.77 (collaborative) and note that the frequency differences between these two corpora are not so great. If we look at "to", we would calculate the normed count in individual texts at 37.09 ($524 / 14{,}124 \times 1{,}000 = 37.09$) and collaborative "to" would be 46.53 ($432 / 9{,}284 \times 1{,}000 = 46.53$). In this case, the normed count in collaborative texts is actually higher than in the individual texts even though the raw count is lower.

In a linguistic analysis, it is also worthy to note not only the potential frequency differences in shared words across the two types of texts but also

Table 8.4 The five most frequent words in a corpus of problem-solution essays written by Thai speakers of English (both raw and normed counts to 1,000 words)

Individual 1-gram	Frequency	Collaborative 1-gram	Frequency
the	726 (51.40)	to	432 (46.53)
to	524 (37.09)	the	425 (45.77)
English	411 (29.09)	and	236 (25.42)
in	372 (26.33)	students	212 (22.83)
and	342 (24.21)	of	182 (19.60)

the use of words that are different in the texts. In this small sample, we not only see differences in nouns ("English" is the third most frequent word in the individual corpus and "students" is the fourth most frequent word in the collaborative corpus) but also differences in function words ("in" is the fourth most frequent word in the individual texts and "of" is the fifth most frequent words in the collaborative texts). Some differences might be related to topic (as with the nouns) but other differences might be related to the production circumstances or relations among participants. Only a closer examination of these features in the corpus can provide us with evidence to support the analysis. Furthermore, Table 8.4 only shows the five most common words; looking at longer word lists would likely show other differences in the corpus that are worthy of analysis and interpretation.

In addition to word lists, the n-gram function can show us potential variation in corpora. As discussed in Chapter 3, n-grams are contiguous sequences of words that can vary in length depending on the interest of the researcher. In Table 8.5, we provide the five most frequent 4-grams in the individual and collaborative texts. We have included both the raw frequency counts as well as the counts that are normed to 1,000 words in parentheses.

The following patterns can be observed in this dataset:

1. No 4-grams are shared between the two groups.
2. All of the 4-grams produced by the first group contain verbs.
3. All of the 4-grams produced by the second group contain at least one (at times two) prepositions (*of*, *in*, and *among*).
4. None of the 4-grams in the first group have prepositions.
5. None of the 4-grams in the second group contain verbs.
6. Overall, the second group seems to have used more 4-grams.

There are many different types of searches that you can do with your corpus. As mentioned in Chapter 5, you should feel encouraged to explore the AntConc program (as well as related literature such as the "read me" files on the AntConc website) to learn about the program. New tools are

Table 8.5 The five most frequent four-grams in a corpus of problem-solution essays written by Thai speakers of English (both raw and normed counts to 1,000 words)

Individual four-gram	Frequency	Collaborative four-gram	Frequency
to solve this problem	27 (1.91)	of teachers in Thailand	31 (3.33)
the first solution is	20 (1.41)	shortage of teachers in	31 (3.33)
there are many solutions	18 (1.27)	addiction among CMU students	25 (2.69)
the second solution is	17 (1.20)	games addiction among CMU	19 (2.04)
to solve the problem	17 (1.20)	teachers in Thailand problem	17 (1.83)

frequently available so you should visit the site from time to time to learn about the new functions and programs.

For example, as mentioned above, an important consideration in understanding the use of any feature (including both word lists and n-grams) relates to the distribution (or dispersion) of a feature in the corpus. A given feature may be frequent, but it is important to make sure that the feature is not used in a few texts at a very high frequency. Although not in a statistical sense as we described dispersion in Chapter 7, you can check the visual of the distribution in AntConc by using the "Concordance Plot" option (see Chapter 5 for details). This function will show you how many different files the given feature occurs in as well as how many times the feature occurs in a single file. This is an easy method to provide a visual representation of the distributional patterns of the feature that you are looking at. Distributional patterns like these can be very helpful in interpreting your results. Seeing the distributional patterns can also help in examining whether your findings for a given feature are, in fact, spread in your corpus or are found in a limited number of texts only. If the latter, you may need to be aware that that language feature is probably used in an idiosyncratic way; that is, it is used only by one or two participants or in only a few of the texts (depending on your unit of analysis).

8.4 Functional Interpretation

As Biber and Conrad (2019) indicate, the final step in a register analysis is the functional interpretation of the results. We mentioned this in Chapter 2; the basic principle here is that language is used in situations and for communicative purposes. Put in another way, language forms have functions and are used to meet the communicative purpose in a given situation. Aspects of different situations can vary, and so do the language forms associated with those situational aspects. According to Biber and Conrad (2019), after we describe the patterns (see above in our mini-project), we need to interpret why the patterns exist the way they do. This step requires reference to both the situational and linguistic characteristics of a text.

For the specific dataset above, we have described some patterns. The fact that no 4-grams are shared by the two groups (i.e., in the two types of texts) could be attributed to certain differences in the situational characteristics; namely the topic, the production circumstances, and relations among participants. Although both groups wrote problem-solution paragraphs, the topics they chose were different; it is possible that these 4-grams are topic-related. However, the n-grams in the individual texts do not seem to be topic-related; they are more focused on providing solutions to the problem. The collaborative group did have 4-grams that mentioned specific problems, but since the individual group did not do this, it is difficult to see how the topic might have influenced the individual writers to mention solutions and the collaborative writers to mention specific problems. Since the time given to write the essays was the same in both the individual and collaborative assignments, the fact that the collaborative group used more types of 4-grams cannot be attributed to the time they may have had to complete the work. The difference might be attributed to other situational variables such as the difference between an exam and an in-class activity or the relationship between participants and the text construction. While the first group wrote the essays individually in an exam condition, the collabo-rative group completed the work as an in-class activity. This is a possible explanation, but it seems more likely that the differences have to do with the production circumstances related to constructing texts individually as opposed to constructing texts as writers are interacting with another per-son to produce a single text collaboratively.

The production circumstances, as one of the situational variables, may also be the reason that one group used verbs, while the other used preposi-tions. In previous register variation studies (Biber, 1988, 1995), particular linguistic features were associated with involved discourse, and others were associated with informational discourse. For example, and among many others, features such as pronouns and contractions were found to be char-acteristic of discourse that is produced in real time (i.e., under time con-straints), as in face-to-face conversations (one of the most involved types of discourse). In contrast, nouns, prepositions, and attributive adjectives were found to be characteristic of discourse where the text could be revised and reformulated, as in academic prose (one of the most informational types of discourse). In addition, results of researching lexical bundles (see definition in Chapter 3) show that conversation has more n-grams that contain verbs, while academic prose packages information through more bundles that contain prepositional phrases (Biber et al., 1999). This pattern is present in our dataset above as well, but instead of being attributed to time constraints, it may be attributed to the fact that collaborative writing influences writers to adopt more forms found in academic writing. That is, when the participants produce language that is the product of collabora-tion (where they need to negotiate aspects of the text such as motivating a problem, structuring their essay, and working on sentence-level grammar and word choice), they seem to use more prepositional phrases. When these same writers produce written texts by themselves, they use more verbs.

8.5 Reporting on Your Project

The previous three sections of this chapter have led you through the steps of analyzing your corpus using a register functional perspective. At this point, you have a well-structured corpus that is guided by a well-motivated research question (see Chapter 5, Section 5.2). You also have a clear methodology for searching for and interpreting your results. It is now time to package your research project so that others can learn about your work. Below, we provide a template for your research paper and include some questions that you can use to guide your research. There are five general parts to a research paper: 1) establishing the research context and significance of the study; 2) introduction and explanation of your data and methodology you used in the study; 3) your results; 4) a discussion of your results; and 5) your conclusion. (Sometimes the results and discussion are found in a single section of the paper but we place them in different sections here.) When writing a paper of this type, you may want to think about writing a small paper for each of these five sections and then putting these sections together for the final product. At the end of this chapter, we also provide you with a sample rubric that can guide your project and give you an idea of how your project can be assessed (see Table 8.6).

8.5.1 Parts of a Research Paper (and Guiding Questions)

1. Research context and significance
   What is the research issue?

   - What is the rationale of the current research?
   - Why was it important to conduct the research?
   - Is the statement of the problem adequate and convincing?

   What other research studies were conducted in the same area?

   - What were the main findings?
   - What are the research questions in your study?

   What are your situational variables?

2. Data and methodology
   Description of the corpus

   - Number of texts; number of words
   - Source of the texts
   - Sub-corpora description (if applicable)
   - File naming system

   Type of corpus research (corpus-driven; corpus-based; combination) and methods used

   - Software programs used
   - Search terms
   - Other methods (e.g., n-grams; word lists)

Table 8.6 Rubric to evaluate student presentations

Criteria	Level 1	Level 2	Level 3	Points
Introduction / thesis	Weak introduction of topic, thesis and subtopics. Thesis is weak and lacks an arguable position	Adequate introduction that states topic, thesis, and some of the subtopics. Thesis is somewhat clear and arguable	Proficient introduction that states topic, thesis, and all subtopics in proper order. Thesis is a clear and arguable statement of position	/4
Quality of information on corpus	Limited information on corpus with lack of details or lack of representativeness	Some aspects of the corpus are well-described but others are lacking (# of texts, # of words, description of sub-corpora, # of words in corpus/sub corpus)	Corpus is clearly described with detailed and accurate description in a table format	/7
Support of ideas / analysis	Limited connections made between evidence, subtopics, and thesis/topic. Lack of analysis	Some connections made between evidence, subtopics, and thesis/topic. Showing analysis	Consistent connections made between evidence, subtopics, and thesis/topic. Showing good analysis	/10
Organization / development of ideas	Paper lacks clear and logical development of ideas with weak transition between ideas and paragraphs	Somewhat clear and logical development of subtopics with adequate transitions between paragraphs	Clear and logical subtopic order that supports thesis with good transitions between paragraphs	/10
Conclusion	Lack of summary of topic/thesis and subtopics with weak concluding ideas	Adequate summary of topic/thesis and some subtopics with some final concluding ideas	Good summary of topic/thesis and all subtopics with clear concluding ideas	/4
Language conventions	Inconsistent grammar, spelling, and paragraphing throughout paper	Paper has some errors in grammar, spelling, and paragraphing	Paper is clear, with proper grammar, spelling, and paragraphing	/8
Citation style	Lack of proper format and limited details with sources missing or incomplete	Some errors in APA format with most sources shown	Proper APA format used in alphabetical order with all sources shown	/2
Total				/45

- Other coding processes (hand coded/counted)
- Normalization

Linguistic features analyzed

3. Results
What are the main findings of the study?

- Charts/graphs/prose presenting what you found in the corpus

4. Discussion of results

- What do you conclude from the findings?
- How do the findings relate to your research issue?
- What are the implications of the findings?

5. Conclusion

- Are the results logically drawn from the analysis?
- Are the conclusion, implications, and recommendations justified by the results?
- What are the limitations of the study and why do you think that they are limitations?

8.5.2 Research Presentation

In addition to the research paper, you may also be asked to give an oral presentation of your research project. For example, you may be required to present your work in ten minutes, leaving five minutes for questions at the end. Your presentation should be accompanied by a visual aid such as various slide show programs such as PowerPoint or Google Slides and/or a one-page handout. Should you choose to do a slide show presentation, try not to put too much text on your slides. For example, you could try to have no more than six lines with each line containing no more than six words. When giving the presentation, try not to read every word on the slide. The slides serve as an outline for your presentation. You should expect that your presentation will be evaluated using the following criteria:

Description of your problem/research issues: Explanation of why your issue is important/a real-world problem
A description of your corpus: Size, number of texts, how it is structured
A description of how you analyzed the corpus: Search terms, commands to the software program you have used
Some results and analysis
A (tentative) conclusion
Format and clarity of your visual aid

References

Biber, D. (1988). *Variation across speech and writing*. Cambridge University Press.

Biber, D. (1995). *Dimensions of register variation: A cross-linguistic comparison*. Cambridge University Press.

Biber, D., & Conrad, S. (2019). *Register, genre and style* (2nd ed.). Cambridge University Press.

Biber, D., Johansson, S., Leech, G., Conrad, S., & Finegan, E. (1999). *Longman grammar of spoken and written English*. Longman.

Chapter 9

A Way Forward

Beyond simply illustrating how searches can be done with a corpus, the purpose of this book is to show how a complete corpus-based project can be carried out, including some of the technical aspects and some basic statistical analyses. As we have discussed many times throughout the book, one can follow a) a corpus-driven or b) a corpus-based (often called corpus-informed) approach to linguistic analysis. In this book, we made an attempt to illustrate both. We showed how we can do a corpus-based study with already identified language features, whether doing a lexical study or searching for the use of particular grammatical patterns. We have also illustrated the notion of a corpus-driven study, as we extracted lexical items (n-grams) from a small corpus and showed what kinds of questions a keyword analysis can answer. While it is relatively easy to carry out lexical studies with corpus-driven approaches (whether you rely on existing corpora or analyze your own corpus), as available tools allow you to extract lexical patterns from the texts, it is quite difficult to apply corpus-driven approaches to do a full lexico-grammatical analysis of texts. The main reason for this difficulty is related to the fact that texts need to be grammatically tagged so that grammatical categories can be extracted from corpora in the same way that specific lexical items are. Tagged corpora cannot only include specific types of grammatical items (such as nouns, verbs and adjectives) but also sub-categories in these different word types (such as concrete or abstract nouns, private and suasive verbs, attributive and predicative adjectives). Some tagging software is available, but there is an increasing need for corpus researchers to gain computational and statistical skills if they want to carry out more in-depth analyses. If you don't have such skills (yet), perhaps the best solution is to continue doing corpus-based studies. You can continue to look for lexico-grammatical patterns that you find interesting, or you can carry out corpus-based studies that rely on the results of previous, corpus-driven studies. For the latter, you would use the findings and apply them to new datasets. We hope that the reference list after each chapter will help you in that endeavor. Without access to tagged

DOI: 10.4324/9781003363309-12

corpora, advanced programming and statistical knowledge, your corpus-driven research will be limited to focusing on word lists, keyword analyses, and n-grams.

Should you choose to expand your corpus linguistic skills, we present below some influential register studies that a corpus-driven approach can offer with the goal of providing comprehensive linguistic characterizations of texts and alternative ways to do keyword analysis in different registers. The purpose of the brief description is to point you to a way forward if you become interested in this type of research.

Unlike the corpus-driven approaches illustrated in this book, more advanced corpus-driven register studies have identified co-occurring linguistic features that have emerged through corpus analyses. While researchers do rely on earlier work to identify functional categories and their associated features before a corpus investigation (Biber & Conrad, 2009: 63), when we are investigating the linguistic profile of a text, it is a mistake not to rely on the constellation of linguistic features. Only this approach would provide us with a comprehensive analysis (as mentioned in Chapter 2). Typically, a large number of lexico-grammatical features are counted at once, and through sophisticated, multivariate statistical methods we are able to see correlations across all of them. Through this methodology we are able to see what linguistic features tend to co-occur and then trace how they are marking different types of texts from different registers.

When we do this kind of research from the beginning (instead of using patterns already identified), the analytical framework applying this empirically based, statistical method to provide comprehensive linguistic descriptions was developed by Biber (1988), and is coined as "multidimensional analysis" of linguistic variation. Among many other works (e.g., Biber, 1995; Biber et al., 2002; Biber et al., 2004; etc.) in which you can read more about the details of this methodology, we highly recommend Biber and Conrad's 2009 book (2019 second edition) titled *Register, Genre and Style*.

Many studies have applied a multidimensional analytical framework as they describe language variation across registers (Biber, 1988; Biber, 1995; Conrad & Biber, 2001; Biber & Conrad, 2019). Typically, and depending on the motivation for the study, researchers have used a multidimensional analytical framework in two ways. On the one hand, researchers use their own corpus to run a new factor analysis (a multivariate statistical method) to identify dimensions of linguistic variation in their own datasets. Examples of this approach include studies that identify dimensions of linguistic variation across registers in English (Biber, 1988) and in languages other than English, for example, Somali and Korean (Biber, 1995), variation in student and adult speech and writing (Reppen, 2001), or dimensions of variation in language use within just one register, for example in university classroom discourse (Csomay, 2005).

On the other hand, researchers may also use an already-existing model where the dimensions (and associated linguistic features and communicative functions) have already been identified prior to the given study. The purpose of these studies is to investigate how their own texts place on the existing continuum of variation and in this sense have a corpus-informed component to them. Examples of these types of studies use an existing dimensional framework, most often referring to Biber's (1988) study, to report on, for example,

> register evolution from a historical perspective (Atkinson, 2001; Biber & Finegan, 2001), variation in language use as it relates to specialized domains such as, author's style (Connor-Linton, 2001), disciplinary language use (Conrad, 2001), intra-textual patterns in medical writing (Biber & Finegan, 2001), or dialect variation (Helt, 2001).
>
> (Csomay, 2015: 6)

Another interesting and new area to explore lexical distributional patterns is applying a type of keyword analysis that is different from what we described in Chapter 3. Ultimately, two fundamentally different approaches emerged in the process of identifying keywords. One begins with the frequency counts of every word in a corpus as a whole – and this is what we showed you how to do in Chapter 3 – while the other is entirely independent of word frequency. Instead, it first considers the dispersion of every word across texts in a corpus (Egbert & Biber, 2019). Several computer programs are available to carry out keyword analysis with the former approach (as we illustrated in Chapter 3) but to our knowledge, no publicly available software is available for the latter but check Laurence Anthony's page as he is constantly updating his free software. At the same time, the latter approach seems to be more geared toward register variation needing large samples of texts as it identifies the representativeness of the "aboutness" of a specific "target discourse domain" (Egbert & Biber, 2019: 77). The latter is a novel approach and something conceptually and methodologically interesting to ponder over, and indeed, try out!

The "way forward" that we have outlined here is most reflective of our own interests and biases in corpus studies and we should end this book by acknowledging many other corpus approaches that are not directly involved in register variation. Some examples can be found in the areas of learner corpora (www.learnercorpusassociation.org/), forensic linguistics (http://www.forensiclinguistics.net/research.html), translation studies (http://corpus.leeds.ac.uk/), and the use of corpora in Natural Language Processing (www-nlp.stanford.edu/links/statnlp.html). These are just a few examples of the many different applications of corpora. We invite the reader, armed with the basic information introduced and practiced in this book, to pursue the areas of corpus linguistics that meet their areas of interest.

References

Atkinson, D. (2001). Scientific discourse across history: A combined multidimensional/rhetorical analysis of *The Philosophical Transactions of the Royal Society of London*. In S. Conrad & D. Biber (Eds.), *Variation in English: Multidimensional studies* (pp. 45–65). Longman.

Biber, D. (1988). *Variation across speech and writing*. Cambridge University Press.

Biber, D. (1995). *Dimensions of register variation: A cross-linguistic comparison*. Cambridge University Press.

Biber, D., & Finegan, E. (2001). Intra-textual variation within medical research articles. In S. Conrad & D. Biber (Eds.), *Variation in English: Multidimensional studies* (pp. 108–123). Longman.

Biber, D., & Conrad, S. (2019). *Register, genre and style* (2nd ed.). Cambridge University Press.

Biber, D., & Conrad, S. (2009). *Register, genre and style*. Cambridge University Press.

Biber, D., Conrad, S., Reppen, R., Byrd, P., & Helt, M. (2002). Speaking and writing in the university: A multidimensional comparison, *TESOL Quarterly, 36*, 9–48.

Biber, D., Conrad, S., & Cortes, V. (2004). "If you look at …": Lexical Bundles in university teaching and textbooks. *Applied Linguistics, 25*(3), 371–405.

Connor-Linton, J. (2001). Author's style and worldview: a comparison of texts about American nuclear arms policy. In S. Conrad & D. Biber (Eds.), *Variation in English: Multidimensional studies* (pp. 84–93). Longman.

Conrad, S. (2001). Variation among disciplinary texts: A comparison of textbooks and journal articles in biology and history. In S. Conrad & D. Biber (Eds.), *Variation in English: Multidimensional studies* (pp. 94–107). Routledge.

Conrad, S., & Biber, D. (2001). *Variation in English: Multidimensional studies*. Routledge.

Csomay, E. (2005). Linguistic variation within university classroom talk: A corpus-based perspective. *Linguistics and Education, 15*(3), 243–274.

Csomay, E. (2015). A corpus-based analysis of linguistic variation in teacher and student presentations in university settings. In V. Cortes & E. Csomay (Eds.), *Corpus-based research in Applied Linguistics. Studies in honor of Doug Biber* (pp. 1–24). John Benjamins.

Egbert, J., & Biber, D. (2019). Incorporating text dispersion into keyword analyses. *Corpora, 14*(1), 77–104.

Helt, M. (2001). A multi-dimensional comparison of British and American spoken English. In S. Conrad & D. Biber (Eds.), *Variation in English: Multidimensional studies* (pp. 171–183). Longman.

Reppen, R. (2001). Register variation in student and adult speech and writing. In S. Conrad & D. Biber (Eds.), *Variation in English: Multidimensional studies* (189–199). Longman.

Available Corpora (Selection)

Bitextes anglais-français corpus: http://rali.iro.umontreal.ca/rali/?q=fr/BAF

BNCweb (A web-based interface to the British National Corpus): http://corpora.lancs.ac.uk/BNCweb/

British Academic Spoken English (BASE): www.coventry.ac.uk/base

British Academic Written English (BAWE): www.coventry.ac.uk/bawe

British National Corpus (BNC): www.natcorp.ox.ac.uk/

Canadian Parliament Hansards: www.isi.edu/natural-language/download/hansard/

CARLA: https://wordbanks.harpercollins.co.uk/

Common Language Resources and Technology Infrastructure: www.clarin.eu/content/language-resource-inventory

Compara: www.linguateca.pt/COMPARA

Corpus of Academic Learner English (CALE): https://blogs.uni-bremen.de/cale/corpusdesign/

Corpus of Contemporary American English (COCA): www.english-corpora.org/coca/

The Corpus of English as a Lingua Franca in Academic Settings (ELFA): www.helsinki.fi/en/researchgroups/english-as-a-linguafranca-in-academic-settings/research/elfa-corpus

EIIDA: https://corpora.aiakide.net/scientext20/?do=SQ.setView&view=corpora

English-Norwegian Parallel corpus: https://tekstlab.uio.no/glossa2/saml?licence=ACA-NCLOC

European Language Resources Association: www.elra.info/en/about/elra/

European Parliament corpus: https://ec.europa.eu/jrc/en/language-tech-nologies/dcep

European Research Infrastructure Consortium: www.clarin.eu/resource-families/parallel-corpora

European Science Foundation Second Language SLA Bank: https://slabank.talkbank.org/access/Multiple/ESF/

French Learner Language Oral Corpora (FLLOC): www.flloc.soton.ac.uk/

ICNALE Learner Essays with Feedback Comments: https://www.gsk.or.jp/en/catalog/gsk2019-b

International Corpus of English: http://ice-corpora.net/ice/index.html

International Corpus of Learner English: https://uclouvain.be/en/researchinstitutes/ilc/cecl/icle.html

Japanese Learner English Corpus: https://alaginrc.nict.go.jp/nict_jle/index_E.html#download

Konan-JIEM Learner Corpus Sixth Edition: www.gsk.or.jp/en/catalog/gsk2019-a

Languages and Social Networks Abroad Project (LANGSNAP): http://langsnap.soton.ac.uk

LeaP: https://sourceforge.net/projects/leapcorpus/)

Learner corpora around the world: https://uclouvain.be/en/research-institutes/ilc/cecl/learner-corpora-around-the-world.html

Linguistic Data Consortium: www.ldc.upenn.edu/about

Michigan Corpus of Academic Spoken English (MICASE): https://quod.lib.umich.edu/m/micase/

Michigan Corpus of Upper-level Student Papers (MICUSP): https://elicorpora.info/

Online Corpus of Academic Lectures: http://www.oncal.sci.waseda.ac.jp/index.aspx

OPUS: http://opus.nlpl.eu/

Russian Learner Translator Corpus: https://rus-ltc.org/static/html/about.html

Sketch Engine www.sketchengine.eu/

Sketch Engine www.sketchengine.eu/guide/setting-up-parallel-corpora/

Spanish Learner Language Oral Corpora (SPLLOC): www.splloc.soton.ac.uk

Spoken Open American National Corpus (SOANC): www.anc.org/data/oanc/contents/

Trinity-Lancaster Corpus (TLC): http://cass.lancs.ac.uk/trinity-lancaster-corpus/

UM-corpus: http://nlp2ct.cis.umac.mo/um-corpus/index.html

United Nations corpus: https://conferences.unite.un.org/UNCORPUS/en/DownloadOverview

Varieties of English for Specific Purposes Database (VESPA): https://uclouvain.be/en/research-institutes/ilc/cecl/vespa.html

The Vienna-Oxford International Corpus of English (VOICE): https://www.univie.ac.at/voice/page/index.php

Index

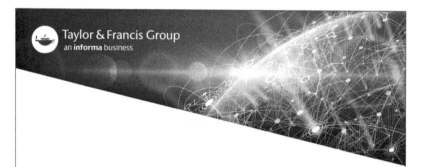

Milton Keynes UK
Ingram Content Group UK Ltd.
UKHW030903141024
449569UK00032B/1850